Marketing/Planning Library and Information Services

Marketing/Planning Library and Information Services

Second Edition

Darlene E. Weingand

1999
LIBRARIES UNLIMITED, INC.
Englewood, Colorado

LIBRARIES UNLIMITED, INC.
P.O. Box 6633
Englewood, CO 80155-6633
1-800-237-6124
www.lu.com

Library of Congress Cataloging-in-Publication Data

Weingand, Darlene E.
    Marketing/planning library and information services / by Darlene E. Weingand. -- 2nd ed.
    xvii, 187 p. 17x25 cm.
    Includes bibliographical references (p. 169) and index.
    ISBN 1-56308-612-3 (cloth)
    1. Libraries--Public relations.   2. Information services--Public relations.   3. Advertising--Information services.   4. Information services--Marketing.   5. Information services--Planning.
6. Advertising--Libraries.   7. Libraries--Marketing.   8. Library planning.   I. Title.
Z716.3.W44   1999
021.7--DC21   99-31433
                                                                      CIP

CONTENTS

ILLUSTRATIONS

INTRODUCTION

USING MARKETING AND PLANNING IN DESIGNING INFORMATION SERVICES

In the first edition of this book, the concepts of marketing and planning were presented as effective managerial strategies. The following paragraphs are taken from the introduction to that first edition as an affirmation that the message is still true; author commentary is inserted as appropriate:

> The concepts of marketing and planning first surfaced in management and business circles. Profit organizations found that the use of strategic planning principles and marketing strategies had a significant effect on profit levels, that ubiquitous "bottom line." Thus, the tenets of marketing and planning have become standard managerial tools within the business community.

Today's business community continues to find these tools essential to effective management practice. Marketing research has definitely replaced the notion of "building a better mousetrap" that was in vogue several decades ago. Customer service has been the mantra of the 1990s and shows every sign of becoming even more influential as we enter the twenty-first century.

> Nonprofit organizations have often been reluctant to engage in aggressive marketing and planning because of a distinct distaste regarding techniques that might be somewhat "shady" and related to "selling"—and therefore inappropriate for public service agencies. It is only recently that recognition of the worth of marketing and planning has emerged in the service sectors.

Nonprofit organizations have become deeply aware of marketing and planning and the potential benefits that are to be gained. Marketing and planning language has entered normal parlance, and the accountability requirements posed by funding authorities are now often presented in strategic planning terms.

In the past few years, several books and numerous articles have been written on planning for libraries and information agencies, ranging from elementary to exceedingly complex. Far less has appeared concerning marketing principles and strategies as applied to the world of information service, and much of what can be found is focused primarily on the promotional aspects of marketing, which is somewhat analogous to describing an elephant by emphasizing its tail. Furthermore, to this author's knowledge, the marketing and planning processes have never been combined into a unified whole.

Since this book's first edition was published, many more books and articles have appeared. However, the definition of "marketing" is still, too often, confused with "promotion," thereby imposing severe limitations on the benefits to be realized. Except for my various publications, the merging of marketing and planning into a single, interactive process remains unique.

The importance of merging these two processes cannot be stressed too strongly. In the past decade, library and information services have encountered technological change on a scale that is unprecedented. Today's information agencies, while continuing the noteworthy traditions that have made libraries such valuable contributors to the growth of individuals and communities, have both the opportunity and the mandate to respond to dramatically shifting client needs.

Certainly the emphasis on change is not only still valid but is perhaps even more critical. In addition, the importance of agency evolution that is in step with community needs is essential if the agency is to move beyond *surviving* to the status of *thriving*. Furthermore, a significant change in this second edition is the introduction of "customer" as a replacement for "client." This deliberate and evolutionary change reflects the true relationship between information agencies and their communities, and it acknowledges that there is no free service but rather service that is financially and socially supported in a variety of ways.

A HERITAGE OF PRIDE— A FUTURE OF CHALLENGE

The heritage of library development is a blend of educational aspirations, the drive for equal access, the democratic tradition, and a search for independence. This blend has fostered the creation and evolution of an institution—the library—that is unparalleled in human culture. The library is an institution that has served its clients with distinction, not always in the ways which some might have wished, but always with purpose and high ideals.

Library development in the United States began with subscription and proprietary libraries that evolved into four basic types: public, academic, school, and special. As the twentieth century has progressed and developments in various technologies have emerged, the nature and character of information access and delivery have changed, presenting new challenges for libraries and library personnel. Libraries often have responded by changing their names to reflect a role shift. Public libraries are now "library and information centers"; school libraries have become "instructional media centers" or "library media centers." Special libraries increasingly face competition from other departments called "information or computer services." Only in academe is the name "library" still the norm and, even there, cost-recovery services are emerging. In addition, increasing numbers of private entrepreneurial information brokering enterprises have entered the world of small business, designed to serve both organizations too small to warrant an inhouse library and individuals who value time more than money when information needs arise.

These two paragraphs attempt to paint the portrait of a dynamic institution that strives to serve its community to the best of its ability ("community" being defined as the group of individuals found in the agency's service area). Some of the dynamism has been natural; other phases have been highly stressful, but there is nothing static about the information world, and the marketing/planning process is the ideal system to help make sense of the changes and design-appropriate responses.

Thus it is that the world of information is undergoing a major face lift. The word "library" is no longer sufficient to define the whole information service. Diversification of mission and roles requires that different agencies assume different titles and identities. At this point in time, an umbrella term is needed to capture the range of this diversity. In this volume, the terms "library," "information service," and "information agency" are all used and the reader is cautioned to interpret these labels in the broadest possible context. The information profession is in such a state of flux and growth that any single label would be limiting.

The interchangeable nature of these terms continues in this second edition. Language naturally reflects reality, and the reality of the information profession is that it is multifaceted and complex.

Furthermore, nonprofit agencies of various missions and descriptions are discovering to their dismay that worthy goals and a desire to serve are inadequate in managerial practice. The focus on what the agency has to offer, and the subsequent promotion of that information, has shifted a full 180 degrees. The institutional focus that will successfully carry an agency into the twenty-first century is one based upon designing services to meet client needs.

Other than the shift from "client" to "customer," this message is still true. The focus must be away from internal operations, except as they support the response to identified needs, and it must shine brightly upon customer expectations and convenience.[1]

It is important to note that the various types of agencies, including libraries, which deal with information as a product have the choice of either competing with or complementing each other. The client needs in this information society are so complex and acute that there is market share for all types of information agencies, but it is through marketing and planning that these market shares can be best determined.

This paragraph suggests two key ideas: the desirability of carving out a market share that is unique (better, faster, and/or cheaper than the competition) and the advantages of partnership (working with one or more organizations to achieve common goals and extend the effect of scarce resources). Both ideas ultimately benefit both agencies and their customers.

> Change is affecting the agency's external and internal environments, and the principles and strategies of marketing and planning are the tools which the manager can use to effectively marshal environmental forces for the betterment of both community and institution. The pressures of the information society require that today's information professionals relate to their clients on an increasingly needs-based level in order to adequately respond to the forces of change. (The term "proactive" means forward looking and in control, and is used repeatedly in this text to focus upon an approach to professionalism that is the opposite of a copying, reactive posture.) No longer can the information agency manager sit back in the traditional easy chair of certainty about the agency's innate value and expect clients to enter through the front door because they "should." In addition, librarians who have historically devoted their talents and skills to a service ethic that has been admirable now find this ethic to be increasingly unworkable in a time of economic constraints.

At the time that the first edition was published, the word "proactive" was just beginning to enter mainstream vocabulary. Now it is standard issue and no longer needs to be explained. The message of taking control of one's own destiny, rather than waiting to react, is even more important today than it was then.

> To work effectively in the emerging diversity of information agencies requires a sense of vision. It is both challenge and opportunity; crisis and frustration. But the rewards far outweigh the stress. The enlightened information professional can minimize the negative factors while creating a dynamic environment for optimal service by building upon the past, seizing the opportunities presented by today, and using the principles of marketing and planning to create a positive tomorrow.

Vision has been underscored and highlighted in the waning years of the twentieth century. Perhaps it has been the prospect of a new millennium, but organizations are actively trying to look ahead and chart courses into the next century that are both imaginative and achievable. Marketing and planning will illuminate this path and help to steer a safe course.

THE STRUCTURE OF THIS SECOND EDITION

The first edition was divided into two main sections: Foundations (three chapters) and Designing the System (six chapters). At that time, this was an appropriate arrangement because the book's content was fundamentally unfamiliar to many readers. Now, however, marketing and planning are more clearly understood, and such an artificial configuration is no longer necessary. In this second edition, the entire process flows in sequence, and the original nine chapters have been expanded into eleven. Some concepts have been merged, and others have been increased in scope.

Chapter 1 answers the questions "What is marketing?" and "How does marketing connect to the planning process?" This chapter looks at marketing and planning as separate systems, but is designed to be an overview of the entire merged process. In chapter 2, the focus is on the marketing/planning team and team building. The argument is made that bringing many minds and viewpoints to bear on creative brainstorming and problem solving is an effective strategy for success.

Chapter 3 expands the creation of a mission to also embrace the development of a vision for the future. As a partner in this enterprise, chapter 4 considers the marketing audit and looks at both external and internal environments, plus environmental scanning. Even if mission and vision are already "known" or assumed, the results of the marketing audit may require revisiting those documents and revising in the light of new data.

In chapter 5, the exercise of developing goals, objectives, and action strategies is combined into an expanded and revised discussion. Types of goals, stages of objective development, ingredients for action strategies, and criteria for evaluation are all part of this discussion. This core of the planning process is essential to producing a marketing plan that works; this new presentation of the essential steps is easier to follow and implement.

Chapters 6, 7, 8, and 9 encompass that set of marketing concepts known as the "4 Ps." Chapter 6 considers information *Products* in this information world. Product design is discussed in detail, within the larger framework of conceptual product models. *Price*, or the cost to produce, is the topic of chapter 7. Both costing and budgeting principles are presented, along with the important intangible factors. Connecting customers and products—the working definition of *Place*—considers channels of distribution and relevant decision factors. Finally, *Promotion*—or communication—is the subject of chapter 9, with special attention to designing the public information plan.

In chapter 10, two approaches to evaluation are introduced: the process evaluation that monitors the entire effort, and the final evaluation that makes decisions about effectiveness. Roles and responsibilities for evaluation are an important part of this analysis. This second edition comes full circle and ends as it begins, with a focus on designing a preferred future. Vision is considered once again, as are customers and information transfer.

Like the first edition, this book is designed to serve as a resource for information professionals in a wide variety of settings, both institutional and entrepreneurial. Students, as prospective professionals, will also find the contents useful in theoretical and practical terms. The concepts presented can be used as framework upon which individual situational and ethical constructs may be placed.

The importance of marketing and planning to the successful and effective information service cannot be stressed too strongly. In a world where change is considered "permanent white water" and increases its pace daily, if not hourly, the role of the information agency becomes increasingly essential to the quality or life in overlapping arenas: personal, professional, societal, economic, and the list goes on. The overwhelming amount of data presented to every customer, everyday, needs to be professionally analyzed and presented in understandable ways. It is an exciting and dynamic time to be an information professional, and this book is dedicated to those who serve, and aspire to serve, in this challenging time.

NOTES AND REFERENCES

1. For a full discussion of customer service, see Darlene E. Weingand, *Customer Service Excellence: A Concise Guide for Librarians* (Chicago: American Library Association, 1997).

Chapter 1

What Is Marketing?—And How Does It Connect to the Planning Process?

What is marketing? Why is it important? What is the relationship of marketing to information service? How is it related to elements of planning? Are the principles of marketing different as applied to the profit and not-for-profit sectors?

These are questions that must be considered carefully in any discussion of marketing and its effect on the operation and growth of information agencies. Systematic marketing and planning are two processes that, until recently, have been largely overlooked as managerial tools. Formerly treated with neglect and indifference, both processes were first adopted in the corporate world and now appear in the nonprofit sector as well.

In the literature of library and information studies, considerable attention has been paid to the planning process in book and periodical publications. While marketing as a concept has entered into the literature, too frequently the term is defined only in the context of publicity and promotion. Further, a symbiotic relationship between planning and marketing adds strength to each process; this chapter is dedicated to the convergence of these processes. First, however, each process will be discussed as an independent entity.

MARKETING AND INFORMATION MANAGEMENT

Marketing is an *exchange* relationship: a process providing mutual benefit to both parties in the transaction. It is an evolving process, one that is influenced by definitions, perceptions, and environmental and cultural conditions and trends. In the past, the concept of "selling" defined marketing; this has now changed dramatically.

Today's interpretation of marketing leans a full 180 degrees from the "selling" definition. Rather than the design of a product, which is then "sold" to a potential public (whether they want it or not!), marketing now consists of an approach to product design that reflects the identified needs of the target populations. In library/ information agency terms, information professionals design a product to meet community needs instead of spending time in the often futile attempt to persuade a reluctant public that they "should" use the library because it is intrinsically valuable.

There is a symbiotic quality to today's view of marketing. Not dissimilar to the Chinese yin and yang symbol, it takes both community needs and library service to become a whole (see figure 1.1). Either of these elements without the other presents an incomplete marketing concept; together, the relationship is defined and the reciprocity well established.

Libraries and information agencies have come from a tradition of being a "public good." Staff have historically been confident that their products had such intrinsic merit that customers would automatically be attracted; they believed that people "should" use the library. This is now yesterday's thinking. The former strategies of telling the community what the library has available and of using persuasion to convince potential users are simply not successful in a world of escalating change, diminishing fiscal resources, and increasing personal options.

In such a world, the pragmatic manager of information services must reexamine the existing relationship between producer and consumer and, using current marketing principles and strategies, forge a new way of thinking and behaving. While this behavior may be unfamiliar, it is necessary, and the theories of marketing are being regarded with increasing seriousness by practitioners in the information professions. Managers with vision are becoming aware that some of the complex issues facing them, such as securing sufficient funding, increasing customer usage, and developing the concept of the library as an essential service, are, in basic terms, marketing problems that can be addressed by using the same marketing strategies that have been so effective in the profit sector. There is a growing awareness that marketing is a valid management tool and, as such, has much to offer information management.

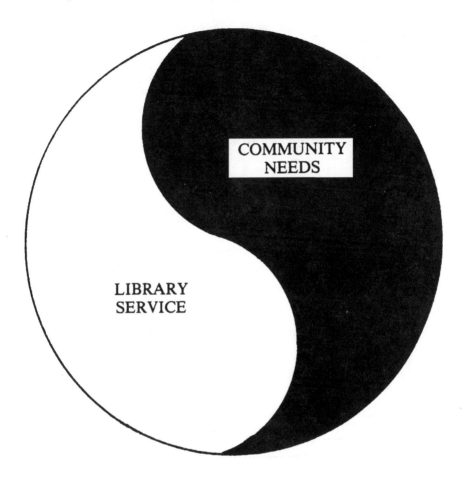

Fig. 1.1. Marketing: The exchange relationship. Reprinted from Darlene E. Weingand, *The Organic Public Library* (Littleton, Colo.: Libraries Unlimited, 1984), 38.

Marketing—A Definition

Philip Kotler offers the following definition of marketing:

Marketing is the analysis, planning, implementation, and control of carefully formulated programs designed to bring about voluntary exchanges of values with target markets for the purpose of achieving organizational objectives. It relies heavily on designing the organization's offering in terms of the target market's needs and desires, and on using effective pricing, communication, and distribution to inform, motivate, and service the markets.[1]

Seven major points should be emphasized in this definition:

1.   Marketing is a *managerial* process involving analysis, planning, implementation, and control.

2.   Marketing is concerned with *carefully formulated programs*—not random actions—designed to achieve desired responses.

3.   Marketing seeks to bring about *voluntary exchanges*.

4.   Marketing selects *target markets* and does not seek to be all things to all people.

5.   Marketing is directly correlated to the achievement of *organizational objectives*.

6.   Marketing places emphasis on the target market's (consumer's) *needs and desires* rather than on the producer's preferences.

7.   Marketing utilizes what has been termed the "marketing mix" or the "4 Ps": *product, pricing, place / distribution, and promotion / communication.*[2]

These seven points emphasize the managerial quality and usefulness of the marketing process. Further, he designed the mnemonic device of "4 Ps" to aid memory retention of the concepts. In the following discussion, Kotler's "4 Ps" will be expanded into "6 Ps" through the addition of two important components: the marketing audit and evaluation. The marketing audit is designated *prelude,* while evaluation is given the mnemonic label of *postlude.*

The Marketing Mix

Prelude—The Marketing Audit

When an information agency enters into a major marketing program, a marketing audit should be conducted. This audit is an independent examination of the entire existing marketing effort (objectives, programs, implementation, organization, and control), plus an analysis of the internal and external environments, for the purpose of appraising the current status of the agency's marketing effort and making recommendations for future action (see chapter 4).

The marketing audit begins with three parts:

1. Evaluating the *marketing environment* of the organization, specifically its markets, customers, competitors, and macroenvironment.

2. Evaluating the *marketing system* within the organization, specifically the organization's objectives, programs, implementation, and organization.

3. Evaluating the major areas of *marketing activity* in the organization, specifically its products, pricing, distribution, personal contact, advertising, publicity, and sales promotion.[3]

Following this close examination of the information agency and its environments, an environmental scan can be conducted to identify trends and possibilities in the near future. Such a scan helps the agency anticipate customer needs in the context of potential change and emerging technologies.

The conclusions of the marketing audit highlight current practices, problems, and opportunities, both in the present and projected tomorrows; the data is then fed into the marketing/planning process.

Product

Product, the first of Kotler's "Ps," can be defined as the output of information agency efforts. Although in the profit sector the product is usually tangible and for sale, the information services product may be more nebulous and may be situated in either the profit or nonprofit context. Kotler's five distinguishing characteristics—quality level, features, styling, brand name, and packaging—can be applied to both the profit and nonprofit sectors.[4]

Examples of the information agency's products include materials (books, videos, recordings, etc.), access channels (reference assistance, cable television interface, computer searches, etc.), and programs (instruction, demonstrations, exhibits, etc.). The range of products offered relates directly to organizational mission and goals. For example, the profit-based entrepreneurial information agency often provides different products than those of a local public library. Once organizational parameters are established, the marketing/planning process can help to delineate the scope of the product mix, the types of product lines, and the numbers of product items (see chapter 6).

Price

Although public library tradition, the "fee versus free" controversy, and the illusion of "free" library service are some of the issues that come to mind when the word "price" is discussed, pricing actually has a far deeper meaning. At its most basic level, price equals cost—the cost required to produce a product (see chapter 7). Cost may be defined as the amount of money or other consideration exchanged in order to provide a service, activity, or function (product). The sum of all costs associated with an activity is known as total cost.[5]

This total cost includes a number of factors:

> *Direct costs*—Those costs readily attributable to a specific activity, such as personnel, equipment, materials, and supplies.

> *Indirect costs*—Those costs not assignable directly to a single activity, such as permanent staff, support services, and operating expenses.

Once a reasonable estimate of cost has been calculated, it must be weighed against anticipated demand for the product. This ratio of cost to demand determines the viability and priority of a product in relation to all other potential products and the known organizational budget. Further, there are two approaches to the analysis of this ratio:

1. In the profit sector, all cost factors (including profit margin) are calculated and a price/fee is set based upon those factors.

2. In the nonprofit domain, the budget is the "known" quantity and all possible products must compete for a share of those finite dollars.

Regardless of approach, the process of cost finding remains the same.

Place / Distribution

This component of the marketing mix consists of the channels that link products and consumers: What will be the customer's access to the product? (See chapter 8.) The point of access can vary widely: a physical location, such as a library or office; the mail; a cable television hookup; a computer connection via telephone lines; or the telephone itself. The distributed product also may take many forms, such as print, audio, video, or computer printout. Rapidly evolving technology continually increases the range of options, both in the product itself and in distribution. Change creates the need for elimination of some distribution channels as well as the opportunity for new development. Advances in telecommunications and miniaturization technologies may require less physical plant space. The proactive information agency needs to cultivate flexibility, knowledge about new trends, and risk-taking ability in order to move creatively into tomorrow.

Promotion / Communication

Promotion, although an important element in the marketing mix, has received more than its share of attention as, too often, it has been considered the definition of marketing. This misconception has led to an overemphasis on promotion to the exclusion of the other partners in the marketing process. In addition, promotion has been based on the assumption, often erroneous, that information somehow exists independently of customer behavior—as an end in itself. This assumption has encouraged the continuance of the perspective of the library as a warehouse/museum/caretaker of materials.[6]

The assumption also fosters the outdated notion that the information product, and in particular the library's products, is so intrinsically worthy that people *should* use it without reference to addressing customer *needs*.

Brenda Dervin has observed:

> The ignorance we have of how people create and use information is more than mere oversight. It is in this arena that we can begin to understand how citizens make sense out of their worlds if they are not using formal information systems and libraries. It is in this

arena that we can begin to understand how to design alternative library activities that can intersect with individuals in more useful ways. [7]

In considering Dervin's statement, it seems logical that information agency activities should be planned on a communication-based model constructed after careful investigation of the information use patterns of the target customer group (see chapter 9). This, of course, meshes well with the promotion/communication component of the marketing mix and with the premise that user need, not provider persuasion, should be the prime mover in the marketing method.[8]

Postlude—The Evaluation

Evaluation is one element that effectively links the marketing and planning processes. There are two aspects to the conduct of evaluation: formative, or process, evaluation that monitors the entire activity; and summative, or final, evaluation that assesses at the conclusion of a project or fiscal year. As each contributes to the effectiveness of the marketing/planning processes, both are needed if the evaluation component is to be complete (see chapter 10).

Formative evaluation is analogous to a compass—it indicates whether the planning and marketing efforts are on course or if a change of direction is needed. Based upon formative evaluation, adjustments continue progress toward the desired goals. Interim decisions are directly influenced by this monitoring activity, and the decision error rate can be greatly reduced.

Summative evaluation, the most commonly recognized type of evaluation, judges final overall effectiveness. This is the aspect of evaluation that occurs at the conclusion of implementation—a final judgment of positive and negative results. Summative evaluation influences decisions on whether certain objectives and/or actions need to be repeated or reworked or whether they were adequately accomplished. This type of evaluation is done at the conclusion of a specified time period (such as a planning year) or an activity. However, evaluation is also an important component of the planning process.

THE PHILOSOPHY OF PLANNING

Why plan? Why go to the expense of using precious time and human resources to develop a planning process? Isn't planning done automatically as part of being a manager? These are very real questions that repeatedly surface when the concept of planning is proposed. It is important to consider these questions carefully, for to succeed as an activity, the motivation or rationale for engaging in that activity must be well thought through.

It is only in the second half of the twentieth century that planning at the corporate level became formalized. There were several reasons for this acknowledgment of the importance of planning. First, companies found that systematic examination of a complex and changing environment produced positive results. The combined knowledge and talents of many people served to identify more readily those variables of opportunity and threat that are the natural byproducts of rapid change. Second, planning forced managers to ask the right kind of questions, such as "What is our business?" and "What are our objectives?" Finally, planning was a logical way to create the future on paper—if what is written is not acceptable, one can erase it and start again.[9]

The discovery of formalized planning by the corporate sector has infiltrated into other arenas of management, including nonprofit agencies. The benefits originally perceived by business have now become part of the managerial consciousness of a variety of organizations.

Planning: A Proactive Guide to Excellence in Management

There is a spectrum of management styles that can be considered as a continuum. The continuum between proactive and reactive management can become a critical factor when the internal and external environments are caught up in rapid change. The closer the information services manager can position the agency to the proactive pole of the continuum, the more opportunity there will be for creativity to be tapped to deal with the inevitable crises of daily operations.

How can this proactive position be attained? The guide to proactive management is systematic and routine planning—the making of decisions within an organized framework as opposed to reactive coping with existing and emerging crises. This framework includes gathering *environmental data*, the development of a *mission statement*, and priority *roles*, the generation of broadly stated *goals* plus measurable *objectives* and *actions*, and *evaluation* of the total process (see chapters 3–5).

As the rate of change accelerates, the insistent clamor of problem situations can become deafening, desensitizing management to any activity beyond the immediate present. Demand and urgency combine to force thoughts of tomorrow to recede from immediate attention. Yet the very existence of crisis is a dramatic reason for incorporating the planning process into the managerial function. This blending of planning and managing can be a strong deterrent to the evolution of a crisis; when advance thought and analysis is routine, problems are less likely to grow to crisis proportions.[10]

Planning can be viewed as a road map. An old Chinese proverb says that if you don't know where you are going, any road will take you there. Engaging in a systematic planning process eliminates this random or scattershot approach to management. When the organizational mission, goals, objectives, and action strategies are articulated, and are based upon careful analysis of customers' needs and environmental realities, then managerial decision making is predicated upon hard data with an eye toward future trends. The destination is charted in advance and decisions can be made that will move the organization toward that destination—alert to potential crises, but always focused on the desired outcome.

Another benefit of planning is the elimination of ignorance—on the part of customers, staff, target markets, and total organization. When a planning team is established, composed of representatives of various target customer and stakeholder groups, lines of communication and commitment are put into place. Direction, function, and purpose are clearly stated as the planning proceeds, and all parties become knowledgeable about organizational intent. The expectations of all involved groups are clarified and the relationship between levels of service and funding sources is articulated.

This dual role of planning, that of road map and of enhanced communication, gives the information services manager the opportunity to orchestrate, rather than legislate, the functions of effective management. Through this analytical and systematic approach to decision making, the manager has the benefit of forethought and design to guide the ebb and flow of present and anticipated events.

Staff Time—A Primary Resource

One of the first arguments countering the beginning of a planning process focuses on the issue of staff time. As economic constraints continually prompt information agencies to tighten their fiscal belts, staffing becomes more thinly spread. The tendency, particularly in libraries, to try to maintain a set level of services with fewer and fewer staff members can be debilitating. Much of this administrative behavior is tied directly to a reactive style of management—one in which planning has never achieved a systematic and routine status.

The proactive manager views planning in a much different light. Such a manager believes that involvement in the process of planning trains staff in managerial skills and helps to meet the need of people in an organization to participate in decision making. In addition, planning helps to establish a communication system and sense of ownership within the organization; staff can use a common language to assess and deal with organizational problems and opportunities.

This concentration on formal planning is not intended to minimize human intuition and judgment. Research in right- and left-brained dominance and contributions to human wholeness has proliferated in recent years. This research has demonstrated that both logic and intuition have distinct and complementary roles to play in human behavior. Carrying this thought into the marketplace, it becomes clear that the collaboration of logic and intuition are needed within the planning process to create an optimal result in the organization. Formal and strategic planning should create an environment in which managers are encouraged to sharpen their intuition and in which time for reflective thought is built into staff responsibilities.

It is interesting, however, that the objective effects of engaging in a routine planning effort are governed in large part by the subjective attitudes of both management and staff. These attitudes make it imperative that a first priority of planning be a careful and thorough explanation of the rationale and the anticipated benefits to the organization as a whole and to staff members individually. Because people appear to be influenced by the notion of *exchange* as the definition of marketing presented earlier, it is important to underscore that *perception of benefit is the true motivator*.

The principles of marketing to be discussed in greater detail in later chapters can be applied with equal success within the organization and beyond. The staff that is convinced of both the intrinsic value and the personal benefit of planning (and marketing) will create a climate in which these coprocesses flourish.

The Relationship Between
What Is and What Could Be

This discussion of the philosophy of planning is not intended to suggest that no planning is currently being done in libraries and information agencies. Quite the opposite is true: Most information professionals would agree that some level of planning is essential, and that planning does necessarily exist. However, as Vernon Palmour, Marcia Bellassai, and Nancy DeWath observe:

> For the most part, the planning that has gone on . . . has not been systematically based on the setting of goals and objectives and the monitoring of progress toward them. Planning has primarily focussed either on the immediate concerns of an [information agency] or an individual parts of the overall operation. Once a pattern of service grows up in an [agency], it tends to go on without review. What has been done in the past determines what is done now and what will be done in the future. The planning process breaks into this comfortable tradition: it reviews the existing service program for effectiveness and balance, establishes priorities, and considers modifications and alternatives to the program.[11]

The publication of the document from which this quotation is cited is indicative of a major shift in the philosophy of the American Library Association (ALA). It is no coincidence that an association such as the ALA moved in the 1980s from rigid standards for service to the concept of planning that is based upon local community needs. This trend continued with the development of a manual on planning and role setting for public libraries, in which the planning process was more clearly articulated and examples of possible roles provided.[12] The evolution continues with the revision of this last work and the recasting of library roles into "service responses."[13] This progression is consistent with the development of planning as a managerial tool upon the organizational scene.

To summarize this discussion on planning, the process of systematic, formal, or strategic planning (the activity, not the terminology, is central here) involves four distinct yet correlated approaches:

1. Planning is a philosophy. It represents an organization's approach to decision making and, as such, demonstrates an organizational priority.

2. Planning is a process. It is a continuous activity, not an occasional event, and involves an ongoing commitment on the part of both administration and staff.

3. Planning facilitates the making of present decisions in the light of projected future events. In this manner, it stands astride the organization with one foot firmly planted in the present and the other placed on the shifting sands of forecasting and anticipation. As the mythical Janus, it looks to the past for knowledge and to the future for inspiration.

4. Planning is actually an amalgam of miniplans, interrelated at several levels. This amalgam considers short-range operational plans as well as long-range strategic plans; it merges departmental plans with an overall organizational mission.

The formalization of planning into a process that looks at the community to be served and designs organizational goals and objectives to correlate with identified community needs is a major step forward in organizational proactive adaptation to a shifting societal structure. The merging of intuitive and analytic thought processes in the planning effort has the potential for creating dynamic organizational change.

There is much to be said for the organizational commitment to formalize planning. Although the focus is generally upon the process and the anticipated outcomes, planning (as with all journeys) begins with a single step. The important decision, which is hopefully made in a consensual rather than an autocratic mode, to engage in systematic planning reveals a great deal about the flexibility and orientation of the organization. It is not a decision to be taken lightly, but, once made, will lead to a better future for the organization.

THE STRUCTURE OF MERGING

Now that marketing and planning have been individually introduced, the next phase in this discussion is to demonstrate correlation between the two processes—that is, to merge the two independent and autonomous processes of marketing and planning into a single system with increased power and effect. There is an appropriateness about the convergence of the marketing and planning processes. Just as the yin and yang symbol was used earlier in this chapter to illustrate the exchange relationship between community needs and library service (see figure 1.1), this same symbol could be used to depict the relationship between marketing and planning. Either of these two processes, while having intrinsic value, is less effective without the other in the sense that each amplifies the power of the other and provides a wholeness of purpose and application. Marketing without planning is an exercise; planning without marketing is a formality. The relationship is somewhat analogous to that of theory and practice: Planning sets the conceptual framework; marketing implements the planning directives and creates an environment conducive to an effective exchange process.[14]

The systems approach is effectively employed in the merging of the marketing and planning processes within the organizational structure. Figure 1.2 illustrates the broad outline of how these separate systems can be linked for mutual enhancement. In this illustration, the marketing audit, incorporating community analysis and needs assessment strategies (of both the external and internal environments), provides the baseline data for both systems. (See chapter 4 for a detailed explanation of the marketing audit.) The planning process is then used for decisions of "where to go" whereas, in parallel construction, the marketing process is used to determine "how to get there." The outcome of the merging of these two systems is the marketing plan, a detailed step-by-step working document that serves as the primary resource for decision making for the duration of the plan.

Whether an information agency is a one-person entrepreneurial effort or a multimillion-dollar library facility, the application of marketing and planning strategies can be a catalyst that promotes effective and creative management. While magic wands only exist in fairy-tale literature, the analogy is not totally fanciful—the principles of marketing can transform a lackluster service into a dynamic and responsive one. The concepts presented in this book should be viewed in a proactive and practical context, not as abstract ideas. Marketing can be viewed as a transfusion of new and vital fluids into an organization, an appropriate image with which to begin.

The diagram pictured in figure 1.3 provides a more detailed breakdown of how the two systems fit together in practical terms. The clear areas represent elements of the planning process; the shaded areas represent elements of the marketing process. The largest evaluation segment—the monitoring function—can be regarded as a part of both processes.

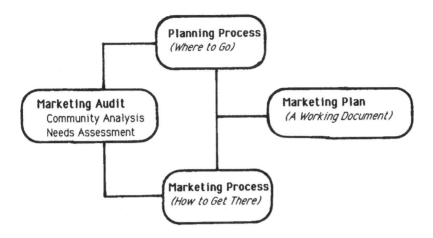

Fig. 1.2. The merging of systems.

To work through this diagram, it should be noted that the processes move sometimes in a single direction and, at times, in both directions. The following sequence is illustrated in the diagram:

1. A *community analysis* of the agency's external environment is conducted.

2. An *assessment* of the agency's strengths and weaknesses (internal environment) is conducted.

3. The data from these two assessments become the *marketing audit.*

4. Following the marketing audit, the organizational *mission and roles* are determined.

5. Once the mission and roles are determined, the *goals* for the time period (one year for the short-range plan and five years for the long-range plan) are established.

6. An *analysis of trends* is made (here depicted as "futures screen" and frequently defined as an "environmental scan"). At the same time, a *vision* for the library's future is developed.

7. In order to move toward the established goals, guided by data concerning trends, alternative sets of *measurable objectives* are created.

8. *Products* are designed in conjunction with the objectives.

9. Analysis of *price/cost* is made to determine product priorities.

10. *Action strategies* (or *action plans*) are formulated for each set of objectives.

11. *Distribution channels* (*place*) are designed in conjunction with the strategies.

12. The action strategies are *implemented.*

13. *Promotion* techniques are designed to implement the strategies.

14. A *final,* or *summary, evaluative review* and updating is made.

Note: A *process (formative) evaluation* monitors progress throughout the operation of the merged systems.

Further discussion of each of the elements in this diagram can be found in subsequent chapters. It is important to emphasize once again that integration of the elements of the two processes, as illustrated in the diagram, provides a more reasonable and consistent approach to the marketing and planning efforts than either system employed independently. The elements flow together easily and naturally, allowing a synchronized response to the "where to go" and "how to get there" questions.

The merged systems approach presented in this chapter is an example of the adage that the whole is greater than the sum of its parts. When marketing and planning are combined into a single process, the resultant management tool is one of power and clarity. It is an innovative approach that can make the difference between an information service that is adequate and one that shines. In the next chapter, the importance and selection of the planning team will be the focus of discussion.

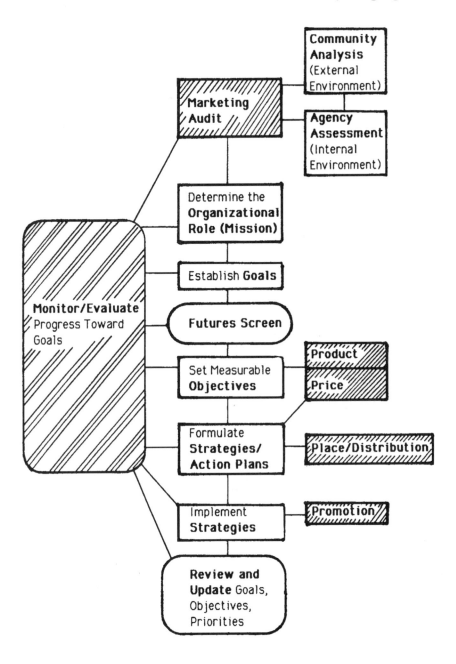

Fig. 1.3. The combined planning and marketing systems.

Scenario for Further Thought: Marketing & Planning

The Rainbow Public Library, serving a community of 30,000, has a staff of two full-time staff (including the director), one part-time clerk, and volunteers. The only planning presently being done is informal and at home. The director recently attended a conference in which marketing was discussed at one of the sessions. Intrigued with the concept, she and staff are contemplating trying to do a marketing plan. What would be the likely result if:

- The planning remains an informal, at-home activity.
- The focus is on the promotional aspects of marketing.
- The decision is taken to engage in a systematic planning process with community involvement.
- The staff rejects the director's ideas because they are already too busy.
- The library board believes that marketing and planning are "trends" and refuse to authorize work time to develop the effort.
- The decision is taken to integrate the planning and marketing processes into a single system.

NOTES

1. Philip Kotler, *Marketing for Nonprofit Organizations* (Englewood Cliffs, N.J.: Prentice-Hall, 1975), 5.

2. Darlene E. Weingand, *The Organic Public Library* (Littleton, Colo.: Libraries Unlimited, 1984), 39.

3. Kotler, *Marketing for Nonprofit Organizations*, 56.

4. Ibid., 164.

5. Philip Rosenberg, *Cost Finding for Public Libraries: A Manager's Handbook* (Chicago: American Library Association, 1985), 5.

6. Weingand, *The Organic Public Library,* 43.

7. Brenda Dervin, "Useful Theory for Librarianship: Communication, Not Information," *Drexel Library Quarterly* 13, no. 3 (July 1977): 24.

8. Weingand, *The Organic Public Library,* 44.

9. George A. Steiner, *The "How" of Strategic Planning* (New York: AMACOM, 1978), 3.

10. Weingand, *The Organic Public Library,* 9.

11. Vernon E. Palmour, Marcia C. Bellassai, and Nancy V. DeWath, *A Planning Process for Public Libraries* (Chicago: American Library Association, 1980), 1.

12. Charles R. McClure and others, *Planning and Role Setting for Public Libraries: A Manual of Options and Procedures* (Chicago: American Library Association, 1987).

13. Ethel Himmel and William James Wilson, *Planning for Results: A Public Library Transformation Process* (Chicago: American Library Association, 1998), 53.

14. Weingand, *The Organic Public Library*, 39.

$\displaystyle =================$ ℭℬ

Before You Begin—Forming a Marketing/Planning Team

ℰ ———————————————

Everyone plans, whether it be a conscious or subconscious activity, formal or informal in nature. In addition, staff often believe that they do market the library—although they typically think only of promotional aspects. The quality of these activities, however, is dependent in large part upon the mechanisms put in place to facilitate the process. In an organizational context, the marketing/planning team (hereafter called the planning team) serves as an administrative advisory and communication conduit, aiding information flow to and from all levels of the organization and between the organization and its community.

WHY USE THE TEAM APPROACH?

The library workplace is one of necessary interdependence between staff and customers, as no library can exist without customers, and customers require the expertise and efforts of library staff to respond to information needs. But within this general construct of interdependence, individual staff members have multiple types of possible behaviors.[1]

There are three major options for individual behavior:[2]

Independent work: I mind my own business and take pride in doing a good job. I feel isolated in my work at the library and look elsewhere for my social interactions. I am careful to perform the duties specified in my job description. (This is the classic example of "It's not in my job description" mentality, a negative force that disrupts harmony in the workplace. While a difficult challenge, such an employee must be made to realize the personal and organizational benefits presented by cooperation—or be counseled to seek employment elsewhere.)

Competitive stance: Organizational rewards go to the winner, and I am in competition with other library employees. I have difficulty trusting other employees and I don't want to depend on others. I want to prove that I am more worthy than others. (This is a clear opportunity for a redefinition of the library's reward structures and the development of a system that will compensate employees for cooperative efforts.)

Cooperative team: I am part of a team in which we all contribute to being as effective as possible. I depend on my team colleagues for support, encouragement, and information. We have good communication and look for solutions that are mutually beneficial. I am loyal both to my library and to my team.

Organizations, whether small or large, derive significant benefit from a participative rather than an autocratic structure. The innovative organization prepared to deal successfully with a changing environment (both external and internal) is an organization that encourages participation from all members of staff. The multiplicity of ideas generated through the application of many minds becomes a significant organizational resource for decision making.

Hundreds of studies conducted by many types of social scientists have documented the impact of cooperation, competition, and independence. The findings consistently indicate that cooperative teamwork, rather than competition or independence, promotes direct communication among people—plus empathy, emotional support, constructive discussion of different points of view, successful problem solving, a high level of achievement, and a sense of confidence and personal value.[3]

Beyond the organizational benefits, although still part of them, lies the notion of ownership. Ownership is the individual staff member's perception and belief that he or she has contributed to the planning and decision making, that the results will be in some part "owned" by him or her. When a person feels like a part of the process, then that person is more willing to live with and implement the decisions that result. This happy outcome does not commonly occur when management style is autocratic and communication is one-way, from the top down.

Ownership is a particularly important concept in relation to stakeholders: Those individuals in the library's external and internal environments who have policy and decision-making authority will either be affected by the decisions to be made or will have some type of vested interest in the organization's future. Involving representative stakeholders on the planning team encourages the development of an attitude of ownership.

Once an information agency has made the basic decision to undertake a marketing/planning process, the most productive step is to select a broad-based planning team to spearhead the effort. At the same time, the agency must perform three additional steps: 1) determine the level of effort feasible for the agency; 2) determine the type and amount of data to be collected through the process of a marketing audit (see chapter 4); and 3) collect, collate, analyze, and synthesize the data. With the members of the planning team appointed (from the stakeholders described above), the scope of effort delineated, and appropriate data gathered, the team is ready to begin its work.

GENERAL CONCEPTS FOR SUCCESS

The planning team is subject to the same positive and negative environmental conditions as are teams or committees of any type or purpose. The first condition to be considered is *mutual respect*. When members of the team accept each other's strengths and limitations within a general arena of respect for individual differences and abilities, the combined attributes can be tapped in a useful way. Conversely, when team members interact in a competitive rather than a cooperative manner, team effectiveness is damaged.

A second condition is *clear expectations*. Each team member should be aware of and knowledgeable about the team's charge and what is expected of the team. In step with clear expectations is the third condition—*common goals*. When the planning team is comfortable with its charge and shares common goals for its purpose, activities, and outcomes, the environment for that team's deliberations is optimum.

Two other conditions must be present in order to facilitate the planning committee's work: *opportunities to communicate* and *the development of a support system*. Communication channels should not be assumed; rather, such channels and the time for their use must be part of the planning structure. In addition, a support system for data collection and feedback should be developed deliberately and made part of the team's operating environment.

Administrative Supports

It is the responsibility of the information agency admini-stration to *clearly establish the responsibilities* of the planning team, the administration, and the staff—and to make these respon-sibilities known to everyone concerned. In addition, a *policy state-ment* supporting the philosophy and concept of marketing and planning should be formulated in order to demonstrate the admin-istration's commitment to the entire operation.

A further and more practical demonstration is also required: *budgetary support* of the venture. As in the U.S. Congress, where a law that is passed but not funded goes nowhere, a policy statement in support of a marketing/planning effort that is not backed by dollars is unlikely to be taken seriously. Administrative involvement and support, both philosophical and financial, for the marketing/planning effort is essential if the outcome is to be successful.

In addition to overall administrative support, pragmatic and specific supports must also be in place. First, there is need for release time from daily duties for staff members who are part of the planning team or who are otherwise contributing to the planning effort. Second, a data coordinator should be appointed to handle the details of data gathering and dissemination to the planning team. Third, mechanisms for internal communication should be estab-lished so that communication channels, flowing in all directions throughout the organization, are in place before the actual planning begins. Finally, staff training will be needed as the marketing/planning effort proceeds. There will be new or different duties, responsibilities, and procedures to be tried and tested; various staff members may be involved with data collection or analysis.

When the general and specific administrative supports are in place, the planning team is ready to begin its serious deliberations.

Composition of the Team

Who should be appointed to the planning team? The needs of each information agency will vary, depending upon local politics and needs. Suggestions of possible categories of persons are given in figure 2.1. Note that "community" refers to the pool of organiza-tions and individuals from which the agency's customers will be drawn. Thus, the community's parameters may be geographical, discipline- or institution-based, focused on specific professionals or business groups, and so forth. The most important criterion for composition of the planning team is that it reflect the interests of those persons or groups who will be affected by the decisions emerging from the marketing/planning process—the stakeholders.

Information agency staff
Information agency administration
Information agency policymakers
    Vice-president
    Governing board
Community representatives
    Business
    Education
    Service organizations
    Department heads
Users/clients
Nonusers
Political groups

Fig. 2.1. Categories for membership on the planning team.

The size of the team will vary according to the community served and the number of identified stakeholder groups. In some communities, the size of the team may be quite large (more than a dozen or so); in others, the team will have fewer members. To encourage individual input and group interaction, a large team will need to be subdivided into working groups, each focused on a different aspect of the marketing/planning process. These smaller groups will undertake short-term responsibilities with a report to the complete planning team.

A planning team advisory committee can also be appointed to serve as a resource to the team and to provide a wider pool of interests and perspectives. Such an advisory committee can be composed of the "movers and shakers" in the community, who will invariably agree to serve if promised no meetings. The key point is that these decision makers agree that they can be telephoned with ideas, problems, and so forth and will then respond with their perceptions and comments. Such an arrangement brings them "on board" and involved with the library's business.

The Schedule of Work

One of the earliest determinations that the planning team must make involves the scope of the marketing/planning effort. The team will need to consider the level of community involvement anticipated, the amount of staff effort that can be expected, the availability of volunteers or other special help for data collection and processing, the need for information for the planning process, the volume of feasible data collection and analysis, and time and monetary constraints.[4]

Once the planning team has carved out the scope of the marketing/planning effort, a schedule of tasks to be accomplished can be prepared. This schedule will include a time line for the total project and its various segments, including assignments of personnel for various responsibilities. Target dates are set for the draft and final reports.

The team also decides what data are to be collected and the methods of collection. Procedures for this data collection are established; methods for processing and analyzing the data are determined. The entire data collection process should be handled with the aid of the data coordinator and whatever other resource people are identified. Because data collection and analysis can be complex, appropriate expertise must be secured in order to assure that accuracy, validity, and reliability are present.

BUILDING TEAM BEHAVIOR

Teamwork doesn't happen automatically. A single leader cannot make it happen. Rather, it results from members paying attention to how they are working together. Issues are identified that are blocking teamwork and the team members work through them. The goal is to consciously develop patterns of working together that all members of the team find challenging and satisfying. Collective self-awareness, openness, and maturity are critical to effective team behavior.[5]

In addition, diverse individuals working together in a team situation can become frustrated if cohesiveness is not created through attention to the general concepts for success stated earlier in this chapter. In addition to those concepts, team members have a right to expect administrative and staff support of their activities, including such basic tasks as taking minutes, photocopying, scheduling meetings, providing information, and so forth. Further, the team needs to have a clear charge and sense of administrative expectations.

For example, is the team to gather data and forward the findings to the director, who will then make decisions? Or, is the team to gather data and make recommendations to the director, who still makes the decisions? A third possibility is that the team gathers data and retains the decision-making authority. These are three very different means of operation and the team members are entitled to know under which model they are to function.

When administrative expectations have been clarified, one of the first team projects will be to assess the situation. By conducting a marketing audit (see chapter 4), both internal and external environments are examined. This examination is the baseline by which the team members identify issues and preliminary goals relevant to their initial efforts. How are these issues and goals determined? What process can be used to generate the creative ideas necessary to move the planning process into the implementation phase? The following types of group process can facilitate the planning team's work.

Three Types of Group Process

One of the most effective mechanisms used in building team behavior is *brainstorming*. Brainstorming is designed to generate the maximum number of ideas, options, and strategies possible within a given time frame. As issues emerge, they are manipulated in as many ways as possible in order to produce the broadest range of creative thought. When no judgments are allowed during this process, the ideas, sparked by creativity, are free-flowing. Differences of opinion are encouraged and individual biases are submerged in the subsequent wave of creative output.

Another example of group process is the *Nominal Group Technique* (NGT). This method elicits participation from every member of the team, regardless of personality characteristics. Each member of the team, in turn, contributes one idea to the entire pot of ideas; the group continues to be polled by the facilitator until all ideas are exhausted. No judgments are permitted; ideas are numbered and written on large sheets of paper and taped on walls around the room. Once all ideas have been listed, each team member selects his or her "favorite five." The facilitator places slash marks on the large sheets opposite the selected numbered ideas. The ideas accumulating the largest scores are then placed on the agenda for further discussion. No ideas are discarded, however; all are retained for future consideration.

A third example of structure for group decision making is the *Delphi Technique.* Whereas Nominal Group is an in-person and face-to-face meeting, the Delphi Technique is anonymous and uses statistical and iterative feedback as major components of its structure. Delphi can be viewed as an invitational conference held via the mail or a computer network; it presumes that the invited members have expertise in the area to be considered. This method consists of several iterative rounds:

1. Round 0 contains a statement of the issue to be considered, phrased as a question, plus supplementary open-ended questions.

2. From the responses to Round 0, a questionnaire listing statements of anticipated change is created for Round 1, and questions are asked about those change statements, such as "How probable is it?"; "When will it occur?"; and "What will be the impact?"

3. Round 2 and any subsequent rounds ask additional questions, allow participants to change former responses, and require participants whose responses fall outside the central 50 percent of all responses either to change their answer or to provide narrative justification.

The Delphi Technique is very useful when individual personality characteristics might interfere and when consensus and/or identification of dissension is sought.

The value of these examples of group process lies in the deliberate effort to evaluate each idea on its own merit. The emphasis on active listening—whether in person or through careful reading of narrative responses—lends credence to the notion that every idea deserves independent consideration.

Putting Ideas into Action

It is the responsibility of the planning team to choose ideas and options most likely to achieve the stated goals and objectives of the organization. This directive should be clearly stated before actual idea selection begins. If ideas are generated that do not seem to support this directive, they should be closely examined and adapted, for innovative recombination of ideas may well further this mandate.

Where differing ideas occur, those ideas need to be massaged to achieve a broad working perspective. In anticipation that real differences may arise that cannot be merged effectively, the team should establish objective criteria early in their deliberations to handle this possibility. Ideas that cannot be reworked, merged, or made acceptable to the planning team should be tabled until some time when conditions may have changed.

Once the decision phase is completed, it is time to implement the ideas. Action plans (see chapter 5) are established for each stated, measurable objective. The responsibility for specific tasks is assigned and a time line of activity developed. The time line for implementation must be constructed so that the pace is comfortable to team members and staff, and within the resources of the organization. The issues that frame the plan should be specific and within workable boundaries. To keep the creative juices flowing, team members should be encouraged to work toward a process of collaboration rather than negotiation. An important overriding philosophy must be to present concerns at all times in a positive, informative manner.

Another responsibility of the planning team is the ongoing evaluation (see chapter 10) of the entire marketing/planning process. Progress must be monitored constantly so that changes of direction can be designed when appropriate and reinforcements, whether economic or human, secured if needed. Success must be measured against the objective criteria of the established goals; although team members' feelings are of considerable importance, they cannot be used as criteria for the purposes of evaluation.

A FINAL WORD

Much has been written in management literature on team building and effective communication. The serious student seeking additional material may well be dismayed by the volume of information available. This chapter has synthesized some basic principles in an effort to chart directions for applying those principles to the management of information agencies. This synthesis can be distilled still further to one paramount concept: The most important ingredient in effective team building is the human one.

Now that the planning team is in place and ready to begin, the first task is to develop a mission and vision for the library/information agency. The next chapter addresses this charge in detail.

Scenario for Further Thought: Planning Team

The Mushroom Public Library, located in a city of 180,000 people, is considering entering into a major marketing/planning activity. The director realizes that someone must collect data and generally supervise the process, but is uncertain how to begin. Advise the director concerning the following possibilities:

1. The director is responsible for the entire effort, assigning tasks as necessary.

2. The director chairs a planning team composed of staff members.

3. The director appoints a planning team consisting of invited members, including agency staff; a member of the board; community representatives from business, education, service organizations, media, etc.; user customers; nonusers; and political groups.

4. The director assigns a staff person to coordinate the planning effort and appoints a planning team representing the groups listed above.

What is likely to happen if adequate administrative supports (both philosophic and economic) *are* and *are not* directed toward the planning effort?

NOTES

1. Darlene E. Weingand, *Customer Service Excellence: A Concise Guide for Librarians* (Chicago: American Library Association, 1997), 45.

2. Dean Tjosvold, *Teamwork for Customers: Building Organizations That Take Pride in Serving* (San Francisco: Jossey-Bass, 1993), 5–6, as quoted in Darlene E. Weingand, *Customer Service Excellence*, 45.

3. Ibid., 7.

4. Vernon E. Palmour, Marcia C. Bellassai, and Nancy V. DeWath, *A Planning Process for Public Libraries* (Chicago: American Library Association, 1980), 20.

5. Peter B. Vaill, *Managing As a Performing Art: New Ideas for a World of Chaotic Change* (San Francisco: Jossey-Bass, 1991), 17.

Chapter 3

Developing a Mission and Vision— Why Exist?

Every organization, and every individual, ultimately needs to answer the question, "Why do I exist?" Although philosophers have wrestled with existentialist-type questions since the dawn of recorded history, the need to know—to come to a comfortable and workable response within one's self—has never diminished. To ignore the question is to drift without purpose or direction through life. To make peace with the question is to create that purpose and direction so necessary to successful living.

A personal sense of purpose is a fundamental element in full human development, but its importance is less apparent on the organizational level. The information agency that works through a deliberate and routine marketing/planning process—beginning with the basic question of "Why exist?"—has a competitive advantage. However, addressing this question is as crucial to the overall health of the organization as it is to the individual person.

ATTRIBUTES OF THE MISSION

Once the information agency has made the administrative determination that an organized marketing/planning effort is fundamental to its effectiveness, the climate is prepared for discussion of the institutional mission. The mission is expressed in two related but discrete ways: the mission statement and the role statement.

The *mission statement* forms the basis for subsequent goals and objectives. It expresses the present and anticipated relationship between the agency and the community to be served. The breadth of its language expresses the philosophy of the agency as it

31

carves out the parameters of service, allowing for fluid movement within the current of a changing society.

The mission statement must correspond to the mission of the parent organization, whether that parent is a corporation, a municipality, a university, or a school. Even when the information agency stands alone as a brokerage, the mission statement should relate to overall community patterns.[1] The mission statement should encourage creative growth of the agency and its staff, giving them meaning and legitimacy vis-à-vis the community served. A clearly worded mission statement makes it easier to identify opportunities and threats as they surface, and relate them to organizational priorities. Systematic management becomes possible because the parameters of operation have been clearly defined.

The *role statement* relates directly to the mission statement, and articulation between the two must be carefully constructed. The role statement is written in the language of action, describing how the agency plans to operate within the planning period to serve community needs. (For example, if a public library's mission reflects a major commitment to information transfer, the role statement may reformat that commitment into the structure of a community information center.) Figure 3.1 presents the list of eight potential roles developed by the Public Library Association (PLA) in 1987. In figure 3.2, the PLA roles are revised and redefined into thirteen service responses. While these roles are focused on public library management, the concept can be recast in terms of any library/information agency environment.

The role statement is concrete, stating who is to be served by specific services and, like the mission statement, shares the attributes of being flexible and of facilitating the identification of opportunities and threats. The role statement takes the more nebulous "why" and redefines it into the structure of "what." It responds to the question, "What is our business?" Peter Drucker states:

> The question "What is our business?" can be answered only by looking at the business from the outside, from the point of view of customer and market. What the customer sees, thinks, believes, and wants, at any given time, must be accepted by management as an objective fact. The customer only wants to know what the product or service will do for him tomorrow. All he is interested in is his own values, his own wants, his own reality. For this reason alone, any serious attempt to state "What our business is" must start with the customer, his [or her] realities . . . situation . . . behavior . . . expectations, and . . . values.[2]

Roles	Description
Community Activities Center	The library is a central focus point for community activities, meetings, and services.
Community Information Center	The library is a clearinghouse for current information on community organizations, issues, and services.
Formal Education Support Center	The library assists students of all ages in meeting educational objectives established during their formal courses of study.
Independent Learning Center	The library supports individuals of all ages pursuing a sustained program of learning independent of any educational provider.
Popular Materials Library	The library features current, high-demand, high-interest materials in a variety of formats for persons of all ages.
Preschoolers' Door to Learning	The library encourages young children to develop an interest in reading and learning through services for children, and for parents and children together.
Reference Library	The library actively provides timely, accurate, and useful information for community residents.
Research Center	The library assists scholars and researchers to conduct in-depth studies, investigate specific areas of knowledge, and create new knowledge.

Fig. 3.1. Public library roles. Adapted from Charles R. McClure and others, *Planning and Role Setting for Public Libraries: A Manual of Options and Procedures* (Chicago: American Library Association, 1987), 49, 4.

Service Response	Description
Basic Literacy	Addresses the need to read and to perform other essential daily tasks.
Business & Career Information	Addresses a need for information related to business, careers, work, entrepreneurship, personal finances, and obtaining employment.
Commons	Helps address the need of people to meet and interact with others in their community and to participate in public discourse about community issues.
Community Referral	Addresses the need for information related to services provided by community agencies and organizations.
Consumer Information	Helps to satisfy the need for information that impacts the ability of community residents to make informed consumer decisions and to help them become more self-sufficient.
Cultural Awareness	Helps satisfy the desire of community residents to gain an understanding of their own cultural heritage and the cultural heritage of others.
Current Topics & Titles	Helps to fulfill community residents' appetite for information about popular cultural and social trends and their desire for satisfying recreational experiences.
Formal Learning Support	Helps students who are enrolled in a formal program of education or who are pursuing their education through a program of home schooling to attain their educational goals.
General Information	Helps meet the need for information and answers to questions on a broad array of topics related to work, school, and personal life.
Government Information	Helps satisfy the need for information about elected officials and governmental agencies that enables people to participate in the democratic process.
Information Literacy	Helps address the need for skills related to finding, evaluating, and using information effectively.
Lifelong Learning	Helps address the desire for self-directed personal growth and development opportunities.
Local History & Genealogy	Addresses the desire of community residents to know and better understand personal or community heritage.

Fig. 3.2. Library service responses. Adapted from Ethel Himmel and William James Wilson, *Planning for Results: A Public Library Transformation Process* (Chicago: American Library Association, 1998).

In a similar fashion, the information agency, through information gleaned from the marketing audit (see chapter 4), must determine the realities of its various target markets and tailor its mission and roles to satisfy the needs and wants of those realities.

Both the mission and role statements must be understood and promoted by all staff members. This implies periodic discussions and review so that communication is ongoing at all levels. In addition, routine reconsideration of the statement is an excellent hedge against potential obsolescence, giving staff the opportunity to update the intent and the language continuously; this updating allows them to stay in tune with current developments and anticipated trends.

CREATING THE MISSION AND ROLE STATEMENTS

Before these statements can be adequately constructed, the marketing audit must take place. Current services must be analyzed to determine who is served and how well. The potential for serving those who do not currently use the information agency must be assessed. In addition, a judgment should be made regarding the commitment of the governing unit, administration, and staff in terms of continuing current service traditions and/or forging into the changeable future.

Following this analysis of the services that the information agency is currently providing (or not providing) to the various target market groups, the agency must examine its present role(s) in relation to the entire community environment. The marketing audit again provides the data upon which these determinations are made.

Special consideration must be given to identifying community information needs and the degree to which those needs are being met by the information agency and by other providers. Information-seeking behavior patterns of agency users and nonusers should be learned in the effort to create a community profile. A careful and thorough assessment of these factors will lead to a realistic calculation of the agency's market share.

The concept of market share will be discussed at length in later chapters; however, it is an important concept to keep in mind. Information agencies serving the broad spectrum of communities, from elementary schools to private corporations, have traditionally made a valiant effort to be all things to all people. This has resulted in significant fragmentation of effort and, particularly when budgets are tight or declining, a dissipation of scarce resources. Today's marketing theory stresses that every provider of a product needs to carve out a unique market share—a portion of the market in which that provider can meet specialized needs that are not being met totally by competitive providers. (The term *totally* is used here because there are many instances in which the target market to be served is large enough to merit the attention of several producers.)

Once the marketing audit has been studied and the agency's potential share of the market has been determined, hard decisions regarding the information agency's mission and role(s) must be made. Possible role components should be ranked using the data from the marketing audit as a guide. The components listed should comprise elements from three major areas: *activity areas, types of service,* and *groups to be served.*

Examples of *activity areas* to be considered include information, education, recreation, and cultural events. Some agencies may elect to concentrate resources on only one of these elements; others may choose two or more. The decision will rest on the identification of market share as it relates to identified community needs and potential duplication of service with other providers.

Types of service to be provided may encompass information services, collection of materials, programming, and outreach. Distribution decisions (see chapter 8) will be predicated in large part upon the types of service selected for inclusion in the agency's role determination. As with activity areas, an agency may elect to concentrate on a single type of service or several.

A third major factor to be added to the mix consists of the target markets, or *groups to be served.* Because no information agency can serve the totality of possible customers, criteria for selection of groups should be established based upon a developed formula of cost/benefit and cost/demand (see chapter 7). The ratio between cost to produce and benefit received is a viable measure that should be incorporated into the decision process.

The mission and role statements, although implicitly "understood" by staff even when not written in a formal manner, will likely change once the data from the marketing audit are analyzed. In many ways, the formal statements are but the final stroke of the pen once the possibly lengthy process of making hard choices is completed. This is not intended to diminish their importance; rather, the emphasis must be placed on process, not rhetoric. However, the absolute importance of clear statements, free of jargon and ambiguity, cannot be overemphasized. The mission and role statements are communication tools—tools that transmit the "why" and the "what" of the information agency's identity to all its target markets, both external and internal. Construction of these statements is a crucial step in the total marketing/planning process. Sample statements can be found in figures 3.3 and 3.4.

Mission Statement of the Greensview Public Library

The mission of the Greensview Public Library is to provide materials and services to fulfill the informational, educational, recreational, and cultural needs of the citizens of Greensview. The library also provides these resources to the people of the surrounding communities and the state. The library subscribes to the principles of intellectual freedom and provides materials reflecting multiple points of view. The library serves customers of all ages and at all levels of need with access to its services through a trained staff, comfortable physical facilities, and appropriate technology.

Roles of the Greensview Public Library

Primary: **Popular Materials Library**
             The library provides current, high-demand materials
             in a variety of formats for all ages.

             Community Information Center
             The library collects and displays information concerning
             community activities and provides meeting room space
             to the community.

Secondary: **Independent Learning Center**
             The library provides materials and services to individuals
             of all ages pursuing a sustained program of learning
             independent of the formal classroom.

             Preschoolers' Door to Learning
             The library provides materials and programs to meet
             the interests and needs of this age group and their
             parents.

Fig. 3.3. Sample mission and role statements.

The Vision Statement

Although the mission and role statements focus on present operations, with some attention to the near future, the vision statement takes the longer view. Where does the agency want to go? What service profile does it aspire to in five to ten years? What goals and objectives and priorities will help to attain that status? The vision statement is an optimistic look at what might be and what should be, and it articulates the information agency's hopes and dreams for the future. In many ways, the vision statement is a scenario written about a future that is hoped for, but not yet realized.

It is important to have a vision statement in addition to the mission and role statements so that the marketing/planning process can have a trajectory into the future. All of these statements are useful and serve unique purposes. They act as separate lenses through which to view library/information agency operations. Each has importance and contributes to a three-dimensional profile of service that spans today and tomorrow.

Vision Statement of the Greensview Public Library

The Greensview Public Library aspires to provide materials in all appropriate formats to its community. It seeks to establish electronic access to library services and resources. In order to offer a comfortable environment for reading, viewing, and listening, the library requires an expansion of the present facility by 50 percent; this expansion will include space for programs and community meetings.

In recognition of a rapidly changing information marketplace, the library intends to provide Internet access for the use of community members; multiple terminals will be part of this access.

In order to more fully serve the needs of its customers, the library seeks to increase its staff complement by three FTE in the professional rank. In addition, cooperative arrangements will be explored with other libraries in the area.

Fig. 3.4. Sample vision statement. This vision statement is presented in a succinct form in the interests of space. Vision statements can be several pages in length. The appropriate length is a local decision.

RECAP: NO ONE RIGHT WAY

It is unlikely that any two information agencies will create identical missions and visions for themselves, for it is equally unlikely that any two communities to be served are exactly alike. The diversity of communities plus the local mix of resources (human, fiscal, and material) create a unique environment. Add to that the diversity in political climates, in competitive providers, and community needs and the portrait becomes still more complex. Although it is a challenge and a creative exercise to establish an information agency in tune with its community, the results are well worth it and may have a major impact on the quality of life.

However, any information agency's mission and vision must be driven by what is learned from the marketing audit. It is not the agency's wishes that are paramount; the focus must be on the customer. In the next chapter, the marketing audit is presented as the baseline for the entire marketing/planning process.

Scenario for Further Thought: Mission & Vision

The city of Greensview has a population of approximately 150,000 people. Located within a three-hour drive of two major cities, it hosts a private liberal arts college. There are many small businesses in the area and a growing high-tech industrial base. Among the information agencies serving this city are:

1. A private information brokerage

2. A college library

3. A public library with six branches

4. Twelve school libraries, three of which are high school libraries

5. Five corporate libraries serving the high-tech industry

What kind of mission and role statements could be written for each of these five types of information agencies? (Specific data from the marketing audits may be improvised.) How do the statements differ? Is there overlap and duplication? How can this be minimized?

What kind of vision statements would be appropriate for each type of agency?

NOTES

1.   "Community" is defined by this author as the totality of real and potential customers to be served by the information agency.

2.   Peter F. Drucker, *Management: Tasks, Responsibilities, Practices* (New York: Harper & Row, 1974), 79–80.

═══════════════════════════ ☞

Chapter 4

The Marketing Audit—Examining the Library's Environments

ॐ ───────────────────────────────

Three terms are used fairly interchangeably to describe the process that analyzes the customer groups to be served: 1) needs assessment; 2) community analysis; and 3) marketing audit. Although they share common elements, the relationship among the three terms is more realistically depicted in figure 4.1. As the diagram illustrates, the needs assessment addresses customer expressed (felt) and unexpressed needs, frequently using survey methodology and/or interview techniques to identify those needs.

Somewhat more encompassing, the community analysis also examines needs, but in the context of the whole community picture. Secondary data concerning demographic statistics and growth patterns lend structure to this process, and primary data collection fleshes out the identified parameters. Community analysis must be viewed as a snapshot in time, representing the community's profile at the time of the examination; it must be recognized that change will be an intervening variable.

The most inclusive of the three, the marketing audit, can be viewed as an "umbrella" that covers efforts to assess client needs and to understand community patterns. (A reminder: "Community" refers to the present and potential customer groups that may be served by the information agency, whether that agency is in the public or private sector.) The external environment is examined on both micro and macro levels, including scanning for developing trends.

In addition to this analysis of the external environment, the marketing audit also analyzes the internal environment of the information agency, thus including the entire environment in its examination. It is to this comprehensive effort, the marketing audit, that this chapter is directed.

Fig. 4.1. Data collection relationships.

THE MARKETING AUDIT
AS THE "UMBRELLA"

The marketing audit has been defined by Philip Kotler as a comprehensive, systematic, independent, and periodic examination of the information agency's total environment, objectives, strategies, activities, and resources in order to determine problem areas and opportunities and to recommend a plan of action.[1]

Each of the terms comprising this definition deserves a closer look:

- Comprehensive— the scope of the audit indicating a commitment to thoroughness

- Systematic—a step-by-step procedure characterized by purposeful regularity

- Independent—a politically autonomous process that is free from outside influence, guidance, or control

- Periodic—happening at repeated cycles, regular intervals

- Environment—the circumstances or conditions surrounding the agency, both within and without

- Objectives—worked toward or striven for, and measurable

- Strategies—plans of action

- Activities—specified and supervised fields of action

- Resources—an available supply that can be drawn on when needed

- Problem areas—situations that present uncertainty, perplexity, or difficulty

- Opportunities—favorable or advantageous combination of circumstances, chance for progress

- Plan of action—process of doing or performing[2]

From this overall definition and the sum of its parts, it can be seen that the marketing audit provides a very complete assessment of the milieu in which the information agency has chosen to operate. With this in-depth, detailed data at its command, the agency's administration will have adequate information for proactive planning and decision making.

COMPONENTS OF THE MARKETING AUDIT

The marketing audit must necessarily be concerned with both the external and internal environments. In addition, the organizational marketing system and an organizational activity analysis must be included, and environmental scanning put into place. Within these components are subgroupings of elements to be considered. For purposes of structure, this discussion will be divided into these five major categories, with appropriate subheadings.

The External Environment

The external environment is everything that is beyond the immediate operations of the library/information agency. It is the outside world that gives the agency its purpose. When examining the external environment, consideration must be given to a variety of factors: demographic, geographic, psychographic, economic, technological, political, societal, cultural, behavioristic, and environmental scanning. Figure 4.2 presents these factors in conjunction with relevant questions that should be considered in the marketing audit. These factors and considerations provide a three-dimensional view of the external environment; they are the composite lens through which the environment can be studied and subsequently analyzed.

External Factor	Related Questions
Demographic	What is the profile of the community in terms of population, age, gender, educational background, income, employment, and so forth? While much of this information is available through public documents, the most current data can only be secured through some type of survey method, keeping in mind that questions concerning age, gender, marital status, and religion may be illegal unless phrased in terms of optional replies.
Geographic	What is the physical arrangement of the community in terms of natural boundaries, climate, and other physical phenomena?
Psychographic	What is the psychological profile of the individuals and groups comprising the target markets? What are their likes and dislikes, their preferences and their biases?
Economic	Although individual and family incomes would be included in the demographic profile, what is the overall community economic health? What are major industries, sources of employment, trends concerning growth/decline? What is the current tax structure, business climate?
Technological	What media hardware is presently owned by members of the target markets (so that appropriate software may be provided)? What is the status of computer networks, cable television, and satellite dishes? What are the communication patterns and capabilities in the community? How are developing technologies being absorbed into both business/industry and personal lifestyles?
Political	What is the policy structure? What is the information agency's relationship to funding sources and to policymakers? How does the power in the community flow? What kind of maneuvering has been done in the past? What has been successful or unsuccessful?

Societal	What is the nature of the social patterns in the community? How do the societal and political structures intersect? What are the relationships among individuals and groups in the community? Is there a common culture or set of values?
Cultural	What intellectual and artistic activity can be identified in the community? Are there gaps? What are the socially transmitted behavior patterns, arts, beliefs, and institutions?
Behavioristic	How do members of the target markets act, react, function, or perform under different sets of circumstances or levels of stress? Can useful methods of prediction be developed and worked into subsequent marketing strategies?
Environmental Scanning	The first nine factors relate to present conditions; scanning looks into the future and attempts to identify trends. What are the anticipated developments over the next five to ten years in each of these factors? How will these developments influence agency operations? How should the agency be responding to potential change?

Fig. 4.2. External environment factors.

The external environment can also be divided into subsets—and each of the above considerations applied to each of the subsets.

1.   The first subset is the *macroenvironment*. At the macro level are those forces that affect the information agency but cannot be controlled by the agency. Both trends and impacts comprise the macroenvironment and need to be worked into the marketing/planning process. Examples include inflation rate, inventions, gasoline prices, postage rates, and legislation.

2.   A second subset is the *microenvironment*. This is the environment that the library can directly influence, where interactive communication can take place. At the micro level is the local community, the information agency's primary service area, including both present

and potential target markets. What are these markets and what is their potential growth or retrenchment? What perceptions and attitudes do members of these market groups hold toward the information agency's product? What decision factors are put into play regarding when to use or not to use the product? What are the needs of the markets, both present and projected? What benefits are sought; what benefits are received? What is the information-seeking behavior of members of these market groups? Finally, what is the estimated rate of change affecting these various groups and what is the tendency of each group to flow with change?

3. A third subset is composed of the *competition*—any and all agencies, businesses, vendors, organizations, or individuals who provide similar products and services. Although competition is frequently viewed in a negative sense, with the attitude of rivalry in striving for the same customer or market, it can also be seen in a more positive light. When two or more providers seek to address the same market, several questions need to be asked: Who or what are these competing forces? What are their strengths? What are their limitations? Where are the areas of duplication? Are there possibilities for cooperation? What are future trends with regard to the competition, the target market(s), the product(s), and the opportunities for cooperation? Finally, given the reality of identified competition, is there sufficient market to support both or all providers? What is the potential for carving out a unique market share?

4. The fourth and final subset is an eclectic mix of *intersects*. They are also *target markets*, not necessarily in terms of being potential consumers of the information agency's products, but rather markets that have some type of impact upon the agency and its products. These intersects include commercial vendors, the total community at large, professional associations, human service and educational agencies, and funding authorities (both public and private). Because these intersects do affect the agency's operation and effectiveness, it is imperative that two-way channels of communication be perpetually in place.

Environmental Scanning

Examining the external environment is like taking a snapshot of what is in place today. However, the marketing audit must also consider tomorrow in terms of alternative and possible futures. Therefore, engaging in environmental scanning is essential to consideration of the external environment.

Everyone does environmental scanning to some degree, even if it is limited to checking a weather report. Many types of scanning are either passive or informal and carried out unconsciously using vague or taken-for-granted criteria. When this passive scanning becomes deliberate and active, it involves a search for specific types of signals or events according to preselected criteria.[3]

A key futures methodology, environmental scanning involves a careful and conscious four-step process: 1) creating a scanning frame, including time span to be considered and potential components (of the external and internal environments) to be tracked; 2) developing a scanning process that involves identifying sources of trend data and continual monitoring; 3) implementing a way of communicating important data that systematically feed into the marketing/planning effort; and 4) evaluating the uses of this intelligence.[4]

The environmental scanning process can be viewed as a continuous loop (see figure 4.3) in which scanning leads to interpretation, followed by acting on the information, making decisions, evaluating data, and ultimately setting goals. Such a loop should not be seen as two-dimensional, however; the loop actually behaves more like a spiral, not covering the same territory but continually moving into a new plane of time.

Environmental scanning is essential if the library/information agency is to operate strategically within a forward-looking mind-set. If scanning is not part of marketing/planning, many phenomena, threats, and opportunities may seem to appear without warning because the early signals were missed. Careful scanning provides the lead time that is so important for responding to developing events. Because issues and trends are constantly emerging, it is essential that the marketing/planning process have scanning as a major component.

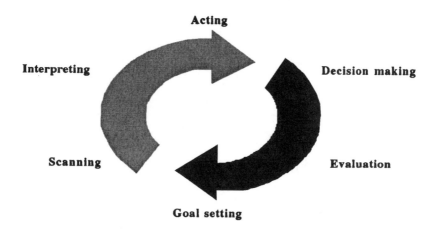

Acting

Interpreting

Decision making

Scanning

Evaluation

Goal setting

Fig. 4.3. Environmental scanning: A loop into the future. Adapted from Richard A. Slaughter, *Futures: Tools & Techniques* (Melbourne, Australia: Futures Study Centre and DDM Media Group, 1995), 25.

The Internal Environment

The internal environment is concerned with the organization itself and consists of every element that comprises the information agency. The careful and thorough examination of the internal environment provides data essential to the marketing audit.

Five discrete yet interrelating components exist within the internal environment. Each component represents an approach to understanding the nature of the organization and its capacity to perform.

1. *The mission.* As discussed in the previous chapter, it is imperative to *know thyself* and to be fully cognizant of the organization's *raison d'être*. An information agency that appreciates why it came into existence and understands its present philosophy of service has a firm base from which to operate. If the level of intraorganizational understanding of this mission is high and anticipated changes are discussed and planned with all affected staff members, then the psychological health of the agency is quite sound.

2. *Goals and objectives.* Every organization needs a road map to travel to the desired destination, and needs to know when that destination has been reached. Chapter 5 will provide more depth, but a brief foreshadowing is necessary in representing this component of the internal environment. *Goals* are global statements of intent and aspiration. *Objectives,* however, are specific and measurable; when accomplished, they move the organization toward stated goals. Both goals and objectives should be written in language that reflects clear marketing objectives and should be ranked in priority order for ease of use. The creation of goals and objectives and the subsequent inclusion of this planning document as an integral part of daily management practice is critical to the internal environment. Product design will be closely correlated to the goals and objectives that are developed. Absence of goals and objectives is a fundamental lack and must be noted as such in the marketing audit.

3. *Resources.* The total resources of an organization need to be identified to accurately assess strengths and limitations. These resources include: a) human—both the people employed as staff of the organization and those to whom the organization has access (including unpaid staff/volunteers); b) financial—the economic assets and liabilities, both actual and potential, that affect management decision making; c) technical—the specialized, scientific, industrial, or mechanical expertise available to the organization; and d) physical—the buildings, equipment, space allocation, furnishings, and other material effects owned or leased by the organization.

4. *Structure.* The structure of an organization through its staffing patterns and lines of communication determines to a great extent how that organization will be able to engage in the marketing/planning process. This structure may be hierarchical, indicating a tendency toward authoritarian management style, or it may be configured in an orbit or matrix mode, thereby facilitating a more participatory management style. Whatever structure and management style are currently in place, however, the reality of that arrangement must be acknowledged and the ramifications assessed during the audit of the internal environment.

5. *Assets and liabilities.* This fifth component of the internal environment is a summation and a synthesis of the first four. The complete internal picture is examined carefully to provide an overall assessment of total organizational assets and liabilities. This assessment must consider the stated mission, the status and/or existence of an active planning process, the entire spectrum of resources, and the organizational management structure. This assessment should then be compared with the assets and liabilities of present and future competitors, keeping in mind potential areas of cooperation and possible duplication.

Once the audit of the internal environment is completed, the next step is the examination of the current organizational marketing system.

The Organizational Marketing System

The information agency may or may not have implemented a formal marketing system. However, it is the rare organization that does not instinctively include elements of marketing in its normal administrative process. The extent of current marketing practice must be identified and monitored as a part of the overall marketing audit.

What is and/or has been the role of marketing in the organization? This fundamental question must receive immediate attention. Although there is a certain overlap with internal environmental analysis, the specific focus on marketing practice is an important element in designing a marketing system.

Three facets of marketing practice should be examined: 1) the philosophy of the information agency regarding the concept of marketing, including administrative commitment to the marketing effort; 2) the distribution of responsibility for current marketing activities, specifying which personnel are accountable for each activity; and 3) the identification of the full range of marketing activities in place both currently and in the past. *A reminder: Marketing practice must be defined as the full range of marketing principles and strategies addressed in this book; if the agency has been viewing marketing as simple promotion, this should be noted.*

Once the role of marketing within the library/information agency has been clearly delineated, a functional analysis of the present marketing system should be initiated. This analysis addresses the following questions:

1. What is the status of routine, formalized marketing/ planning within the organizational structure? Does a planning process exist? Is it pro forma or does it have real impact upon managerial decision making? How often does the process take place or is it ongoing? Who participates? Who is responsible, and for what segments of the process?

2. What are the lines of control regarding the marketing/ planning process? As above, who participates and who is responsible, in what areas? Are there specific reporting procedures in place? What is the information and communication flow?

3. How do marketing activities interact with other aspects of management? Since management must deal with the diverse functions of planning, controlling, directing, organizing, and staffing, marketing activities necessarily will have points of intersection with each of these functions. Are these interactions positive and supportive or are they competitive and self-defeating? How well do members of staff relate to each other and to marketing philosophy and activities? Is a spirit of cooperation present?

4. Is there a marketing information system in place that provides a continuous stream of marketing research? Is there a mechanism in place to continually update the marketing audit? If so, do present communication patterns effectively distribute this information? If not, are there plans to develop and implement such a system?

5. How are products developed in the information agency? Who makes the decisions? Upon what criteria are these decisions based? Do the procedures of product development also include product phasedown and product elimination? Is the concept of the normal product life cycle (see chapter 6) accepted by management and other members of staff?

When the functional analysis of current marketing activity has been completed, the focus shifts to two final aspects of the organizational marketing system: resource allocation and plans for major changes. The first, resource allocation, assumes that, because a finite amount of resources (human, economic, and physical) exists at any given time, these resources are subject to a rationale for allocation. That rationale must be examined carefully so that recommendations for adjustments can be included in the overall marketing audit.

The second aspect refers to plans for major changes that are already in the works. These changes may be early on in the conceptual stage or at some point in the implementation phase. It is imperative that proposed changes be included as part of the marketing audit even though the major effects may be part of the long-range picture (see "Environmental Scanning" section earlier in this chapter). Changes do produce preliminary impacts, and the anticipated outcomes will affect marketing decisions for today and tomorrow.

Organizational Activity Analysis

Once the overall organizational marketing system has been identified and assessed, the focus once again shifts—this time to a closer look at organizational activity concerning the various market segments for which products have been designed. The central four components of the marketing mix are examined according to the present organizational activity and the specified target markets.

The first component of the marketing mix to be considered is _product_ (see also chapter 6). The type and extent of present products offered to the various target markets should be determined. In addition, potential products that may be added—and those that may be phased out—need to be included in this assessment. Finally, trends that affect either the volume or the quality of the products must be added to the equation in order to achieve a realistic evaluation of the current product situation (see section on "Environmental Scanning").

The second component is _price_ (see also chapter 7). What is the cost to provide each product, including direct and indirect costs? Are actual fees being charged and, if so, how are they determined? Are there potential fee-based products to be considered as part of the product determination? The bottom line here is the ratio between cost and benefit—as it affects the information agency (producer) and the customers from the target markets. It is not inconceivable that a high-ticket product (in terms of cost to produce) may also have a corresponding high benefit and/or demand, whereas a product that can be provided at relatively low cost may be perceived as generating minor benefits.

Place (or distribution) is the third component of the marketing mix to be examined, including existing distribution channels and potential alternative channels (see also chapter 8). Changing societal needs because of the increasingly fluid nature of the workplace and the development of significant new technologies are creating a strong demand for innovation in channels of distribution. In addition, the concept of access is crucial: Both physical access and time access must be addressed. Once the concept of access is factored into the total marketing equation and tempered by the cost/benefit assessment, priority rankings of products to be provided can be determined.

The importance of customer identification of both product and distribution channels leads to the fourth component to be discussed: *promotion* (see also chapter 9). Promotion can be defined as communication, with the messages to be communicated traveling along a variety of communication channels selected from the spectrum of media possibilities. Clear promotional objectives should be written for each potential communication channel, then budget allocation decisions can be determined based upon these objectives. Communication channels are selected to correlate directly with target markets; the effectiveness both of the channels and the message is continuously monitored. (It is worth noting that when communication/promotion is done effectively, it becomes correspondingly easier to engage in successful fundraising.)

The organizational activity analysis contributes an integral piece of the total marketing picture and, if conducted in a thorough manner, highlights the gaps and blank spots that need to be filled in when the marketing plan is designed.

THE PROCEDURE FOR CONDUCTING A MARKETING AUDIT

Thus far in this chapter, the elements that comprise a marketing audit have been discussed in detail. There is a four-step procedure or structure into which these elements can be inserted. This structure is firm, yet flexible, so that it can be molded to the local situation of each library/information agency.

1. *Determination of what elements will be covered.* This is a local filtering of the totality of ideas presented in this chapter. Three filters are required:

a. Consideration of the depth of coverage of each element. This depth will hinge in large part upon the next two filters, but rests upon the additional factors of availability of human resources, frequency of the audit, observed change in the community, and any other local condition that would have a significant impact upon the operation of the library/information agency.

b. A common understanding among agency staff members concerning their expectations of what the audit will provide. It would be unrealistic for one staff member to expect detailed statistical analysis to support a predecision while another staff member expected the audit to provide data that would facilitate a decision-making process, and a third staff person regarded the whole effort as a useless exercise!

c. Consideration of resources available to conduct the audit. As stated earlier, resources include financial, physical, and human components. A realistic appraisal must be made of what the information agency can accomplish with the resources at its disposal.

2. *A preliminary review of the audit process.* This review begins the formative (or process) evaluation that will monitor the audit from beginning to end. Starting with the common understanding of expected outcomes mentioned above and with the corollary agreement that elements of the audit may be redefined as it proceeds, this mechanism of formative evaluation prevents the audit from derailing midstream; it keeps the process moving in the right direction.

3. *Data collection and analysis.* Two major types of data will be collected and analyzed. As both types are important to the audit process, they should be gathered with care and precision.

a. Secondary sources. An information agency is in the ideal position to gather data from secondary sources because this is truly its area of expertise. Documentation from a host of federal, state, and local agencies can provide extensive demographic, economic, and geographic data, as well as a good deal of other data concerning the external environment. The agency's own reports will provide additional valuable information.

b.   Primary source material. Once the secondary data has been collected (so that potential duplication can be avoided), it is time to secure primary data. Primary sources provide original data not previously gathered. Surveys are commonly used to tap the primary sources of the community; these can be done via mail, telephone, or through interviews. Numerous human and print resources are available to aid in the design and implementation of a survey; however, because questionnaire construction can be a difficult and specialized skill, it is recommended that outside expertise be consulted. It is vital that primary source material be sought as this is an early, vital link to potential target markets.

4.   *Report preparation and presentation.* The final part of the structure is the formal analysis and synthesis of all available data and the preparation of an informational report. This report should be both written and oral, presented in summary form to management and to the entire staff. It can also be desirable to present the results of the audit to funding authorities, the community at large, and/or representatives of specific target markets.

The marketing audit may seem to be an exhausting endeavor. When it is done within the parameters of the library/information agency's resources and kept to an appropriate scale, it can become a genuine opportunity to capture a snapshot of the agency and its environments and cast considerable light upon the decisions to be made in the creation of an effective marketing plan. The marketing audit is not an optional activity; it is the cornerstone of the marketing/planning effort.

Once the data from the audit is in hand, the time has come to establish goals and objectives. If the library/information agency is to operate in a proactive manner, setting goals and objectives and implementing action steps will provide the necessary structure. Chapter 5 considers this component of the marketing/planning process.

> ## *Scenario for Further Thought: Marketing Audit*
>
> The marketing audit has value for any type of information agency. The city of Woodsville, U.S.A., has a population of 150,000. It contains several manufacturing companies, many small businesses, the home office of a major insurance company, and a small liberal arts college. It is near a major metropolitan area, enabling many citizens to live in Woodsville and commute to work.
>
> Among the information agencies located in Woodsville are:
>
> 1. The Woodsville Public Library and its eight branches;
> 2. The Woodsville College Library;
> 3. The InfoMart, a private information service;
> 4. The corporate library for the Alpha Insurance Company;
> 5. The Woodsville School Library Media Center.
>
> For each of these information agencies, consider the following questions:
>
> Who should do the marketing audit?
>
> What information will be needed?
>
> When in the budget year should the audit be conducted?
>
> How often should the audit be done?
>
> Where will the information come from?
>
> Why is this information necessary? How will it be used?
>
> How can the audit be fitted into the library/information agency's normal routine?

NOTES

1.   Philip Kotler, *Marketing for Nonprofit Organizations*, 2d ed. (Englewood Cliffs, N.J.: Prentice-Hall, 1982), 185.

2.   Definitions adapted from *American Heritage Dictionary*, 2d college ed. (Boston: Houghton Mifflin, 1982).

3.   Richard A. Slaughter, *Futures: Tools & Techniques* (Melbourne, Australia: Futures Study Centre and DDM Media Group, 1995), 43.

4.   Ibid., 170.

Chapter 5

Goals, Objectives, and Action Strategies—A Road Map to an Effective Future

&) ─────────────────────────

When contemplating an automobile journey between Chicago and San Francisco, the wise motorist will gather appropriate maps and plot the route to be traveled. Just getting behind the wheel and starting to drive might land the motorist in Texas or Canada, rather than the desired destination of California. This planning activity is essential to a successful journey. In fact, the entire process of planning can be generalized into the metaphor of taking a journey.

A FIRST STEP: SETTING GOALS

In today's complex, multifaceted world filled with terminology and jargon, the concepts of goals and objectives can become entangled in a web of confusing definitions. Although no consensus exists in defining what goals and objectives truly mean and how they differ, this chapter defines goals as global statements of intent and objectives as measurable, concrete statements that will move the organization closer to achieving its goals.

Given this set of assumptions, goals may be viewed as aspirations, as statements of purpose. They are not defined in measurable terms and are not necessarily attainable. As such, they may remain in place for years, needing little modification, yet providing a focus for directed activity. Goals are fluid, yet reasonably constant, adapting well to changing conditions. Prime movers for policy development, they are grounded in the philosophy presented in the mission statement and steered by the hopes expressed in the vision statement. Goals give direction, set forth priorities of service, and form the basis for the development of practical and measurable objectives.

If planning can be compared to taking a trip—to the journey between the present and the future—then the setting of goals can be viewed as determining a final destination. Goals enable the information manager and the staff to move collectively in the same direction, expending energy and resources in a systematic, organized manner. Therefore, goals allow the information agency to express where it is headed and facilitate the choice of roads by which to reach the destination.

An example of a goal statement written in global language is "To provide timely and accurate information to the identified target markets." Such a goal statement may be established as a beacon to guide service quality, with the specific intent of its parts modified over time by the development of measurable objectives. In other words, some of the language of the goal statement allows for variance in interpretation in response to current community conditions. This language includes:

> *timely*—does this mean a week, a day, an hour, or several minutes?

> *accurate*—in terms of last year, last week, or today?

> *information*—what level or depth?

> *target markets*—may change repeatedly

As specific objectives are developed for the operational (annual) and long-range (five-year) plans, the meaning of the language in the goal statements will be clarified.

Types of Goals

Three basic types of goals need to be developed: 1) product management goals; 2) resource management goals; and 3) administrative goals. These areas reflect the primary divisions of information agency operations and, as such, require related sets of goals.

Product Management Goals

Goal statements that provide the direction for the agency's product development are understandably critical to effective operation. Securely anchored in the information gathered in the marketing audit regarding both external and internal environments, these goals form the framework for objectives that will specify types and levels of services, products to be provided, and the target markets to be served. These goals support product development at all states of the product life cycle (see chapter 6) and channel the flow of product viability as products are created, grow, peak, decline, and phase out.

The importance of goal setting to the flow of product viability cannot be emphasized too strongly. Without clear direction, ineffective products may linger indefinitely, absorbing agency resources that might otherwise be reallocated to new product development. Conversely, goals that pragmatically reflect current and projected environmental realities can provide strong leadership in producing new products and enhancing present healthy products.

Resource Management Goals

The ability to reach toward product management goals is predicated in large part upon the support provided by resource management goals. These goals are primarily concerned with agency operations and relate to funding, materials, staffing, and product distribution. Resource management may often seem like an exercise in stretching an ever-shrinking canvas over an increasingly larger frame, but with adequate goals in place to give purpose and direction, resources are expended only in avenues that lead to fulfilling the organizational mission.

Funding. No library/information agency can function without funding. In a time of shrinking budgets and fiscal difficulties, there is increasing pressure to seek financial support from multiple sources, both public and private. Funding goals will chart the direction of the agency's efforts to identify present and potential funding opportunities. Examples of possible directions include establishing a foundation, pursuing donations and/or bequests, grantsmanship, and collaborative efforts.

Materials. Goals referring to materials acquisition, maintenance, and weeding should relate directly to target markets (customers sharing one or more common attributes). In addition, the range of formats encompassing the increasing spectrum of media options must be carefully monitored to accommodate the variety of learning styles preferred by members of those target markets. Acquisitions goals should cover the scope of acquisition policy, areas of acceptable overlap, and timeliness of purchase and receipt. Access goals may be found in both this category and the distribution category, referring to issues of speed and convenience. Goals correlated to specific output measures, such as availability and use per capita, as well as turnover rate, also fall within this category. Finally, goals addressing the conditions for removal of material should also be included.

Staffing. Because more than 70 percent of the library/information agency's budget is typically expended on staff salaries and benefits, a well-thought-out set of goals related to staffing is critical to effective management. Human resources management might well be considered part of the total resource management goal set, but the amount of dollars involved mandates individual consideration.

Personnel management goals, to be successful, must be predicated not only upon efficiency but also upon the development of genuine regard. Administrators who deliberately and conscientiously formulate staffing goals that encompass both organizational aims and human development aspirations create a dynamic, positive climate.

Staffing goals should incorporate statements regarding employment conditions and the working environment, plus channels and opportunities for interpersonal and intraorganizational communications. Rationale for present and projected organizational structure may also be included. In addition, expectations regarding performance and productivity should be clearly articulated. Finally, particularly important in this time of increasing change, goals for staff continuing education and in-service training should be identified.

Product Distribution. Although distribution is a marketing component that justifiably deserves its own chapter (see chapter 8), goals are needed to chart direction for decision making. There are many distribution factors to be considered when formulating goals:

> How adequate are present facilities, including physical sites, electronic linkages, and any other channels of distribution? Should goals be written to improve present facilities or build new channels?

> How do the target markets presently use these facilities—how well, how often, at whose convenience? On a scale of one to ten, how accessible is each channel to the target market it is designed to serve? Should any channels be phased in and/or phased out? Do newly developed technologies present any potential opportunities to be considered? Should goals be developed to make changes in present distribution outlets?

> What is the cost of operating each distribution outlet? How does that cost relate to cost/benefit? Should goals be written that specifically target cost/benefit issues?

When these factors are analyzed (as part of the internal environment component of the marketing audit), goals for distributing products based upon the most favorable cost/benefit ratio can be determined.

Administrative Goals

Administrative goals are organizational in nature, incorporating both internal and external relationships. Organizational structure is appropriately addressed, as well as present and anticipated cooperative activities with other governmental or resource agencies. Although the language is highly qualitative in nature, it serves to demonstrate the organization's commitment to designated activities and proposed actions. Future plans as well as current operations should be defined—with the overriding purpose of facilitating all previously formulated goals.

Environmental Scanning—Future Screens

In all goal-setting exercises, it is imperative that emerging trends be identified. Normally included as part of the marketing audit, environmental scanning (referred to as "futures screens" in figure 1.2) results need to be deliberately factored into the goal-setting process. Scanning consists of the gathering of data upon which projections of future developments and changes may reasonably be based.

Two approaches to scanning should be considered: The first, as a component of the marketing audit, deliberately seeks out data that would forecast potential trends and changes in the internal and external environments (see chapter 4). At this stage, the scan becomes part of the process in developing the organizational mission and serves as a part of the groundwork for goals development.

The second approach filters the developed goals through alternative scenarios and statements of "What if . . ." such as:

What if conditions (economic, societal, political, etc.) remain the same as they are today?

What if conditions change markedly in a positive direction?

What if conditions change markedly in a negative direction?

The results of such scenario building is the construction of multiple sets of measurable objectives for each goal statement. When this additional task is incorporated into the marketing/planning process, there are fewer surprises, since potential events have already been carefully planned for in a calm and rational way that is devoid of the emotional impact of impending crisis.

Summary—The Process of Setting Goals

These attributes of setting goals are grounded in a set of commonsense assumptions. First, ideas must come forth from the entire staff, not just one individual. In order to foster the necessary "ownership" in the process that will ensure its successful implementation, all staff need to feel involved and that they are part of the total effort. Levels of authority and hierarchical charts are deterrents to creative thought; "blue sky" brainstorming and team building are infinitely more productive.

Second, outside constituents and anyone who will be affected by the goal-setting activity must be kept informed and also have an opportunity to provide input into the process. Acceptance from these groups is critical to success; everyone affected by the decisions should be involved in the process.

Third, the cause-and-effect relationship between overall organizational goals and those of units or departments within the agency need to be in the planning team's awareness at all times so that appropriate correlation can be maintained.

Finally, reality needs to be a continual yardstick against which to measure ideas (not at the brainstorming stage, but at the successive evaluative stages). This is not intended to discourage dreaming, for dreams are often the stuff of which tomorrow's reality is made. However, when goals are to be translated into concrete and measurable objectives for the one-year operational and five-year long-range plans, the reality yardstick must be pulled out in order to keep within the realm of reasonable possibility.

David Hussey underscores the importance of an effective goal-setting effort:

> [Goals] . . . may be regarded, when used in appropriate manner, as the beacon which on a dark night welcomes the fishing fleet into the safety of the harbor; used badly they can become the sweet singing sirens which lure the unsuspecting vessel to founder on the rocks of disaster.[1]

Once organizational goals have been developed, it is time to create the parallel sets of objectives suggested by the "What if . . ." questions. These objectives should be designed to organize the information agency's resources in the most effective way so that the agency moves toward achieving its goals. The administration that follows its objectives in decision making and as a guide in daily operations has made gigantic strides toward achieving its organizational mission.

THE ANATOMY OF OBJECTIVES

Because goals have been defined as global in nature, it follows that objectives, to be able to achieve goals, must be specific and measurable. Stated in terms of an expected outcome and written in clear language, objectives are more focused than goals. In terms of attributes, objectives:

> are *specific* in terms of tasks, results, time, and responsibility;
>
> are *measurable* so that ongoing evaluation can easily determine when the objective has been attained;
>
> contain a *time line* indicating when the objective is due to be completed;
>
> identify *responsibility*: the person or persons who are responsible for seeing that the work described in the objective has been accomplished;
>
> imply that *organizational resources* will be expended in support of realizing the objective;
>
> have a *short term* in which to be accomplished;
>
> are *consistent* with organizational goals and other objectives;
>
> use *language* that is precise, verifiable, and understandable;
>
> use *action verbs*, verbs that suggest improvement of existing [library] services or movement in new directions.[2] (Examples include: [to] apply, begin, construct, develop, establish, gain, improve, maintain, provide, seek, etc.)

Cyril Houle sees objectives as essentially rational, being an attempt to impose a logical pattern on some of the activities of life. Further, he views objectives as practical and preparing for action—pluralistic actions that are designed to lead to the completion of the stated objectives. The ultimate test of an objective, he feels, is not validity but achievability.[3]

Following this approach, we see clearly that obscurely written objectives (which are usually based on insufficient preparation) will not aid an information agency in becoming a more effective organization.

Objectives—Milestones Along the Way

Objectives may be viewed as landmarks or milestones that mark progress on the journey to the goal. Each goal is supported by a series of objectives and, as introduced earlier in this chapter, there should be parallel sets of objectives that can be plugged into the planning process in response to changing environmental conditions (see figure 5.1). Rather than work with a single set of objectives that may be forced into major revision if either positive or negative environmental/economic impacts should occur, it is more efficient to construct parallel sets of objectives from the beginning of the planning process. In this way, if and when an unforeseen impact does occur, contingencies have already been considered, enabling decisions to be made based upon logic rather than upon the emotion of the moment.

When the construction of objectives is done in this flexible, future-oriented manner, the process is essentially rational and practical. The objectives then become tools that relate closely to changing environments and are a purposeful expression of organizational intent.

It should be recognized that objectives, while they should correlate with each other to be consistent, may also from time to time put limits upon each other. By the very nature of making choices—where choosing one option necessarily precludes selecting others—the developing of objectives is discriminative. It is entirely possible, if not likely, that selecting one course of action may well rule out selecting other potential courses of action. It is rather like an exercise in juggling—keeping the balls labeled "contingency objectives" and "possible objectives" all aloft until the planning process determines the preferred course of action.

Goal: To improve access to materials

Objective Set 1 (Little environmental impact)

1. To purchase a microcomputer for in-library use by fall 2000 (director)

2. To begin planning process for building addition by summer 2000 (director, board, committee to be assigned)

3. To increase overall reference requests by 5 percent annually over the next five years (reference staff)

4. To increase the circulation of materials by 5 percent annually over the next five years (all staff)

Objective Set 2 (Negative environmental impact)

1. To seek funds from local service clubs by purchasing a microcomputer by fall 2000 (director/board)

2. To rearrange interior of library by fall 2000 (all staff)

3. To increase overall reference requests by 3 percent annually over the next five years (reference staff)

4. To increase the circulation of materials by 3 percent annually over the next five years (all staff)

Objective Set 3 (Positive environmental impact)

1. To purchase three microcomputers for in-library use by fall 2000 (director)

2. To begin planning process for new building by summer 2000 (director, board, committee to be assigned)

3. To increase overall reference requests by 10 percent annually over the next five years (reference staff)

4. To increase the circulation of materials by 10 percent annually over the next five years (all staff)

Fig. 5.1. Examples of parallel sets of objectives.

Stages of Objectives Development

There are four stages that are distinct, yet blend together as the marketing/planning process proceeds. These stages may seem like common sense, but it is vital to acknowledge that they do indeed exist. They include: 1) preliminary development of objectives—a first cut; 2) tentative selection of objectives; 3) revised objectives, after all data, including trends, have been analyzed; and 4) final objectives.[4]

Preliminary Development of Objectives

It is frequently useful for the three basic types of goals (see page 58) to be initially treated separately. Preliminary discussion and writing relative to each goal set may be assigned to a small group for report back to the entire planning team. This delegation of the overall task helps to disperse the idea generation and the work assignment into subteams of manageable size for concentrated effort.

Tentative Selection of Objectives

Once the first cut has been made, each of the three work groups assesses the ideas presented and selects those objectives that will be forwarded as recommendations to the full planning team.

Revised Objectives

After receiving the recommendations of the work groups, the planning team considers each objective within the context of the overall mission and goals of the organization. The objectives are individually modified so that they accurately reflect organizational direction and the reality of environmental conditions.

Final Objectives

Once all the objectives have been appropriately modified, the planning team considers them as a group, again within the context of the overall mission and goals of the organization. The objectives are arranged in priority order from most to least important. Although each objective is individually important, this importance will increase or decrease in relation to: 1) the assessed ratio between cost to produce and demand (see chapter 6); 2) the economic and human resources of the information agency; and 3) the current and projected political/societal environment.

An important note to remember is that all goals and objectives are written in sand, not stone. Planning team members need continually to remind each other that every part of the marketing/ planning process is subject to change. In addition, as has been mentioned repeatedly, all persons who will be affected by either the marketing/planning process or the results of the process *must be involved* in some way in the process.

Checkpoint Questions

James Hardy recommends that the following questions be asked during the objective-setting exercise:

> Is the objective designed to contribute directly to the achievement of one or more of the library/information agency's goals?
>
> Is the objective feasible in light of internal and external constraints?
>
> Is the objective measurable?
>
> Are the results observable?
>
> Were those who are accountable for achievement involved in the objective?
>
> Were those who will be affected by the objective involved in the process of formulation?
>
> Does the objective have a challenging quality?
>
> If the objective involves other departments/units, was it established collaboratively?[5]

The key words in this list are *contribute, feasible, measurable, observable, accountable, affected/involved, challenging,* and *collaboratively.* If these key words are kept in mind—even posted on a bulletin board—while planning is underway, the planning team should remain on track.

The Influence of Product and Price

The final development of objectives is tied directly to decisions made concerning products and price (see chapters 6 and 7). The ratio between the cost to produce each product and the market demand for each product must be calculated and fed into the marketing/ planning process. This ratio becomes a cost/benefit yardstick, a useful tool in the planning team's deliberations. In other words, it may be an erroneous assumption to believe that because a service is expensive, requiring a considerable amount of the agency's resources, it should be a low priority as potential objectives are being discussed. If there is a correspondingly high customer demand for the product under consideration, the ratio may be very good indeed.

Conversely, the service that is relatively cheap to provide may not be cost-effective at all, if customer demand for it is low. Careful analysis of both cost and demand for each present and potential product is a wise use of the planning team's time and energy. (For further discussion, see chapter 7.)

In the discussions that precede final decision making in the selection of objectives, it is helpful to apply the cost/benefit yardstick to the range of possibilities, ranking both the goals and the possible objectives in order of priority. The data secured through the marketing audit will provide the input necessary to develop the yardstick and to create this ranking. Product development and organizational effectiveness will be greatly enhanced.

The development of goals and objectives frequently turns out to be a convoluted, time-intensive activity. During the entire effort, a system of monitoring evaluation should be in place. Without this conscious attention to evaluation of the process as it proceeds, direction may become misguided or even lost. The planning team should carry as part of its charge the responsibility for ongoing monitoring of its efforts so that work remains on target.

Summary—Objectives As Milestones

Earlier in this chapter, objectives were compared to milestones as indicators that the journey toward organizational effectiveness was proceeding in a timely and appropriate manner; this analogy continues to be accurate. It is crucial to enlightened management practice to set objectives that are measurable and specific determinants of organizational progress toward identified goals. Objectives serve as reachable points to strive for and, once reached, as identifiable intrinsic rewards for accomplishment. In working through the process to achieve the satisfaction of success, the entire organization reinforces its sense of purpose, creating a destiny for its future. The benefits far outweigh the efforts and frustrations that accompany the journey; it can be a most worthwhile trip.

ACTION STRATEGIES—
THE PLAN OF WORK

Once the mission, goals, and objectives have been developed by the planning team, it is necessary to identify the various tasks that will accomplish the stated objectives. Goals and objectives proclaim where the organization is going; action strategies specify precisely how to get there. As with objectives, each action is tagged with a time/date by which it will be completed and the name of the person(s) who will be responsible for completing it.

The image of a staircase (see figure 5.2) can be helpful in understanding the relationship between the design and implementation phases of the marketing/planning process. During the conceptual stages of the process, the planning team moves down the staircase, step by step, beginning with the marketing audit, continuing with formulation (or revision) of the organizational mission, setting goals and objectives, and concluding with the development of action strategies. Decisions concerning product, price, place, and promotion occur at each of these steps.

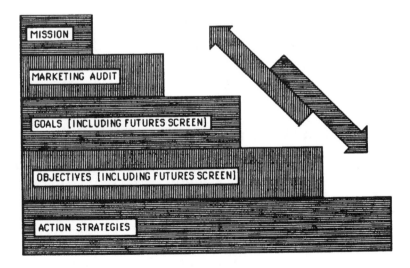

Fig. 5.2. The staircase concept in planning.

During the implementing stages of the process, movement on the staircase reverses—action strategies are completed, which accomplishes the objectives, moves the organization closer to reaching its goals, responds to the needs identified in the marketing audit, and, in turn, fulfills the organizational mission. This staircase analogy can be useful for positioning the concepts presented thus far. It not only clarifies the relationships among the stages of the marketing/planning process, but also determines relative order and sequence.

The Manner of Movement

One of the dictionary definitions for action is "manner of movement"—a definition that seems particularly appropriate, for the movement taken in implementing an action strategy not only has an intrinsic movement of its own, but also moves the information agency that much closer to completing one of its objectives.

Strategies, however, consist of possible actions that are designed to support goals and objectives that either move the agency further along in the direction in which it is already headed or assist in a change of direction. A strategy represents a twofold approach:

1. It is a *process* that encompasses both objectives and actions, serving as an overall *design or pattern* within which tactical moves are made.

2. It is the *series of specific tactics / actions* that accomplish the objectives and are supportive of the overall strategy.

Therefore, the actions that are selected as part of a strategy help to achieve the library/information agency's current goals and objectives and are both realistic and politically astute.

John Hutchinson states that "strategy involves the planning and direction of projects or campaigns, while tactics deal with the operational aspects of moving or handling forces or units. Strategic decisions encompass the development of broad directions and comprehensive plans needed to move an organization toward the achievement of its principal goals. Tactics are the specific means by which these goals can be attained."[6]

Although members of core management, whether represented by a few individuals or a management team, are most directly involved with the responsibility of strategy formulation, all members of staff are expected to carry out the tasks of strategy development and the implementation of tactics. The overall strategy design, created for the entire organization, is concerned with interrelationships; tactics/actions are often developed for particular functions or subunits. Throughout the development period, the management process should be facilitated.

Critical Ingredients

One of the critical ingredients for the planning team to consider is the accommodation of *assumptions and variables*. Assumptions are factors relative to both external and internal environments that the planning team can state with near certainty. Variables include unpredictable factors and, therefore, cannot be forecast with more than educated guesswork. As both sets of factors will strongly affect the process and outcomes of the action strategies, an awareness of their existence is necessary to realistic planning.

A second critical ingredient is *methodology:* the development of action strategies through group process. For the purposes of this chapter, the definition of group process extends far beyond the limited experiential boundaries of the planning team, including all persons and constituent groups who will be affected by the resultant decisions. The solicitation of a wide range of ideas results in maximum diversity in the thinking applied to the problem-solving activity. This forum for encouraging creativity produces not only a healthy supply of ideas, but also identifies targets of opportunity because of the eclectic mix of persons involved in the process. The Nominal Group Technique described in chapter 2 is a useful methodology for gathering a broad range of ideas.

Once all ideas have been generated, a screening process is introduced to help evaluate ideas and rank them in priority order. After current and anticipated opportunities and threats are assessed, multiple sets of actions are established to respond to environmental scenarios that would be "ideal," "likely," and "worst case." The use of environmental scanning (futures screens) to project trends is an important component in this part of the process; the construction of scenarios that look backward in time from some future point may prove to be a useful exercise. (Figure 5.3 presents an example of such a scenario, titled after the Roman god Janus, who looked both backward and forward.) When the scanning activity is completed, the group leaders and those taking notes then submit written reports to the planning team for final consideration.

The Janus Scenario

It is now the year 2010.

Describe the changes in your community over the past ten years.

Discuss the library/information agency's response to events in this time period.

Compare the results of this scenario-building exercise with currently emerging goals and objectives.

Should present plans be altered in order to more closely move toward directions identified in the scenario?

Fig. 5.3. Example of a "Janus Scenario."

A third critical ingredient is the planning team's conscious attention to the *relationship between the sets of action strategies and the four central Ps* of the marketing mix. As action strategies are designed, they should deliberately reflect decisions regarding product, price, place/distribution, and promotion. Because maintenance of the logical flow between the planning and marketing processes is crucial to long-term success, every effort must be made to keep the flow both stable and productive.

The Process of Developing Action Strategies

Activities may be developed by subunits of the planning team or by the entire team working as a committee. Responsibilities may also be assigned to staff members, as both management and staff must be continuously involved because they will be affected by the decisions to be made and charged with carrying out those decisions.

A planning team may generate many activities for each objective. This is to be expected as the committee discusses the list of library/information agency objectives that has been formulated. Objectives should be discussed in their order of priority to the organization, a ranking accomplished at the objective-setting stage. In addition, both the objectives and the subsequent activities need to be directly related to the data gained from the marketing audit so that the process is predicated upon facts and not suppositions.

As the development of activities is more of an art than a science, it may require brainstorming sessions to develop all the possible activities for an objective. Creativity and innovation should be encouraged when initially suggesting action strategies. No idea should be discarded or restricted in the first round because it is not immediately feasible.[7]

There are numerous references in the literature to the Nominal Group Technique, a systematic procedure for eliciting the maximum number of ideas from a group on a nonjudgmental basis (see chapter 2). This technique, which has real merit, should be considered for inclusion in the action strategies process. When judgment can be consciously suspended and all members of a group are compelled to actively participate (such as in Nominal Group), then the flow of ideas is significant. The tendency to dwell on the traditional and the familiar is overcome by the sheer volume of ideas. Overlap is not a problem, because the technique has a subsequent ranking and synthesizing component. Related options may be combined later into larger units of activity.

As with the creation of objectives, time lines and responsibility designations are appended to each action statement so that the team—and the administration and staff—will know who is in charge and when the action is due to be completed. Clarity of language is important, as readily understood activity statements will give all staff members a sense of direction and a better knowledge of individual purpose within the organization. Further, evaluation is a relatively simple matter when objectives and action statements are stated in these clear, measurable terms.

Although the topic of evaluation is treated more fully in chapter 10, it is important to acknowledge the relevance of process (formative) evaluation in the entire activity generation exercise. The planning team should consciously measure each proposed activity against the double-sided yardstick of a benefit assessment and impact—what are the benefits and potential impacts both to the library/information agency and to its customers, and how does the ratio between price/cost and benefit/impact compare with similar ratios established for other possible activities? Additional criteria for evaluation are discussed in the next section.

Forecasting can play a useful role in process evaluation as well as in the setting of goals and objectives. Potential incremental gains and losses as a result of each planned activity should be analyzed in the light of projected trends and environmental conditions, and the determinations factored into the yardstick of benefit/impact. In this manner, both present and anticipated reactions can be dealt with in the planning stage.

A necessary caveat to keep in mind during process evaluation is this: <u>No individual</u> or group preference (that is, based upon personal like/dislike or perception of gain/loss) should be allowed to influence the planning team's deliberations. All decision making must be based solely upon data from the marketing audit and projected trends.

Criteria for Evaluation

As action strategies are proposed, within an overall "game plan" strategy, the monitoring piece of evaluation needs to be in constant attendance. There are three basic criteria proposed by Palmour, Bellassai, and DeWath against which to measure strategies:

1. Their contribution to the library's goals and objectives;

2. Their costs in staff time and other resources; and

3. The effect on other services or programs of possible diversion of resources to the new activity.[8]

The first criterion is straightforward, a logical continuation of the thought processes that this work has attempted to stimulate. Referring again to the staircase concept in figure 5.2, the development of action strategies should be regarded as the pivot point in the marketing/planning process in which the direction of activity shifts from the conceptual to the actualization mode. Planned movements are translated into real-time events as the process that has been so carefully formulated now becomes a series of three-dimensional actions designed to accomplish specific objectives and move the information agency toward achievement of its stated goals and mission.

The second criterion relates specifically to price: the total cost in fiscal and human resources to produce a product or activity. Because there are generally several routes by which to reach an objective, proposed action strategies need to be assessed not only for expected outcomes, but also in terms of the cost involved. The decision to proceed should be grounded in both perspectives; the ultimate evaluation needs to reexamine once again, with the excellent vision of hindsight, whether the cost of the journey was worth the trip.

The third criterion also focuses upon price—this time, the price/benefit ratio discussed in chapter 7. This ratio applies here in relation to other possible uses for the organization's resources, aiding the planning committee in its constant effort to see the "big picture"—each action in the light of the total marketing/planning effort. Not only is the cost per action calculated, but the relative benefit vis-à-vis every other proposed action. This criterion can be viewed as the "conscience" of the planning team's deliberations at this stage.

There are also other criteria to consider beyond the three proposed above. Effectiveness can be measured in several ways: internal consistency, consistency with the external environment, appropriateness in view of resources, acceptable degree of risk, appropriate timetable, and workability.[9]

Internal Consistency

The strategy reflects consistency with the information agency's goals, objectives, policies, and other strategies. Little or no conflict is present. This examination of relationships to these other aspects of the marketing/planning process is a critical step in strategy design.

Consistency with the External Environment

Managers need to be ever aware of the changing environment in which the agency operates, paying note to both current conditions and future trends. It is fair to state that today's manager must plan with the mind-set that he or she is shooting at a perpetually moving target! Strategies developed in concert with both internal and external environments are far more likely to achieve positive long-term results. It is also very useful to develop sets of alternative action strategies (analogous to designing sets of parallel objectives) in order to accommodate possible environmental shifts and changes midstream. This proactive approach to strategy formulation allows for logical, clearheaded decision making that is not influenced by the high emotion produced in a time of crisis.

Appropriateness in View of Resources

The strategy should be assessed in terms of the personnel, equipment, supplies, and operating budget necessary to implement it successfully. If the human and economic resources needed to do the task adequately are not present, the strategy has little chance of being pursued effectively. In addition, the concept of cost/benefit discussed in chapter 7 must be factored into the discussion on resources so that action strategies may be appropriately arranged in priority order. The philosophy of excellence also has an important role, as product development (see chapter 6) must focus on this key point.

Acceptable Degree of Risk

The level of risk that can be realistically accepted is also tied irrevocably to the available resources. In addition, careful analysis is mandatory before ventures involving high risk (and therefore potential resource involvement) are begun. Although big returns are often associated with high-risk activities, a realistic appraisal should be the first step. In many cases, price considerations are critical to the decisions on level of risk.

Appropriate Timetable

The total planning effort, particularly the goals and objectives, should be kept in mind before time lines are assigned. Sufficient time for implementation is one of the key building blocks in successful strategy development.

Workability

What is the likelihood that the strategy will work? An honest response to this question can provide the psychological check and balance necessary to increasing the probability of success. This is truly the "bottom line" of strategy formation. Everyone wants positive results.

Summary—Action Strategies

Finally, action strategies may be implemented on an agency-wide basis or experimentally in a pilot project, depending upon the action's projected effect upon the organization. If a major shift in policy or distribution of agency resources will result from an action strategy, the pilot approach may be more practical until sufficient evaluation data is available for ascertaining the probable success of the endeavor. If, however, the action strategy is designed to accomplish a critical objective and the time line does not allow for experimentation, then agency-wide implementation is the most realistic course to take.

Action strategies are the nuts and bolts that hold together the various parts and pieces of the marketing/planning process. Clear evidence of a viable process, they are deliberate steps toward realization of the agency's goals. Developed with a view toward where the agency has been, is now, and should be going, action strategies nurture organizational objectives into full bloom.

However, as illustrated in figure 1.3, establishing goals, objectives, and actions (the planning elements) must operate in concert with making decisions on the 4 Ps of marketing: product, price, place, and promotion—discussed in detail in the next four chapters.

Scenario for Further Thought: Setting Goals

Millette College Library, serving a small liberal arts college in a suburban community, was about to celebrate its centennial year. The college librarian, who had just been appointed, was astonished to learn that a planning process had never been part of the administrative role. In order to enter effectively into the library's second hundred years, the librarian appoints a planning team consisting of library staff, faculty, students, and other college personnel. The team has decided on this working mission statement: "The Millette College Library serves the academic community of the college. Materials will be collected to support the curriculum, which is fluid to reflect the needs of a changing society."

What are some possible goals that the planning team might consider in each of the three types?

Product Management Goals
Resource Management Goals
Administrative Goals

Scenario for Further Thought: Objectives

The MidTown Information Agency, which just opened for business in a small suburban area adjacent to a middle-sized city, wants to create a formal marketing/planning process with its new employees. Accordingly, the firm's president appointed a planning team with broad representation from various target market groups and a series of goals were developed for the agency. What would be the likely outcomes if:

- One set of objectives was created for each goal and . . .
    1. Little environmental change occurred in the first year;
    2. A major industry relocated to another state;
    3. Urban development resulted in an influx of new small business;
    4. Two new shopping malls were approved by the city council;
    5. State support of local government was significantly curtailed?

- Three sets of objectives were created with economic contingencies in mind, and the five situations listed above occurred?

- The planning team did/did not monitor its progress?

- The objectives, written in global terms rather than specific, did not include time and responsibility lines or expected outcomes?

- All staff members were not involved in the process?

Scenario for Further Thought: Action Strategies

The Instructional Media Center in Alphaville has begun an organized marketing/planning process. After moving through the initial stages, the planning team is about to initiate discussion of possible action strategies. What is likely to occur if the following situations are true?

- The planning team consists of three teachers and the library media specialist.
- The IMC's mission has been identified as a resource to support the instructional purpose of the school, but many teachers continue to send students to the IMC in order to get them out of the classroom.
- The planning team voices ideas, but one individual dominates the discussion.
- No consideration is given to the resources necessary to support each activity.
- Each strategy is carefully assessed to consider its benefit and impact upon the IMC and its customer groups.
- Time lines are established, but no responsibility is designated because several planning team members assume that this is the library media specialist's responsibility.

NOTES

1. David E. Hussey, *Introducing Corporate Planning*, 2d ed. (New York: Pergamon Press, 1979), 34.

2. Ted Despres and Diane Driessen, *Writing Goals and Objectives, Long Range Planning for Public Libraries,* Occasional Paper Series 1, no. 5 (Columbus, Ohio: State Library of Ohio, n.d.), 3.

3. Cyril O. Houle, *The Design of Education* (San Francisco: Jossey-Bass, 1976), 140–41.

4. Donald E. Riggs, *Strategic Planning for Library Managers* (Phoenix, Ariz.: Oryx Press, 1984), 35.

5. James M. Hardy, *Corporate Planning for Nonprofit Organizations* (New York: Association Press, 1972), 65.

6. John G. Hutchinson, *Management Strategy and Tactics* (New York: Holt, Rinehart & Winston, 1971), 49.

7. Mike Jaugstetter and Janice Williams, *Strategy Development and Evaluation, Long Range Planning for Public Libraries,* Occasional Paper Series 1, no. 6 (Columbus, Ohio: State Library of Ohio, n.d.), 1.

8. Vernon E. Palmour, Marcia C. Bellassai, and Nancy V. DeWath, *A Planning Process for Public Libraries* (Chicago: American Library Association, 1980), 70.

9. Riggs, *Strategic Planning for Library Managers,* 46–47.

Chapter 6

═══ ‎C3

The Library's Products— Heart of the System

‎❧ ───────────────────────────────────────

There are eleven chapters in this book, each dealing with the various facets of the marketing/planning process. It may seem curious to the reader that product, which is justifiably termed the "heart of the system," falls almost in the center. This is a correct placement because much has to be accomplished before decisions regarding product design can be made, and, on the other side, there is much to be done in carrying out those product decisions.

The importance of this chapter cannot be stressed too strongly. The success of all other marketing and planning efforts hinges directly upon the quality and excellence of the products that are designed. There is simply no substitute for a top-notch product; inferior or inadequate design will scuttle the most meritorious planning and marketing strategies. Customer trust must be earned; in order to earn trust, it must be deserved. To deserve customer trust, products must have quality and long-range durability. It is therefore imperative that product design be given adequate time, attention, and resources so that the library/information agency's products will be not only effective responses to community needs, but also excellent in their own right.

THE PRODUCT APPROACH IN AN INFORMATION WORLD

In the for-profit sector, of which some information agencies are a part, the definition of product is relatively straightforward. Products in this domain tend to be tangible items, with a fixed cost to produce. Components of this production cost frequently include observable elements, such as raw materials, labor, and so forth. Overhead charges are added on top of the fixed costs and a profit margin is assigned. The result of these calculations is a unit cost, which is then ascribed to the product as a charge per sale (see chapter 7 for a fuller discussion of pricing).

This view of product development is concrete and reasonably straightforward. In an information agency operated on a profit basis, such as that of a private information brokerage, the same process applies; the product, however, lies in the realm of information and services rather than only tangible goods. There still remains a "bottom line" in terms of costing out and recovering cost for services in order to keep the agency in operation.

In the not-for-profit sector—where the majority of library/ information agencies operate today—these principles still apply to product development. As the identities of the various products tend to be largely intangible, the mandate for cost recovery gives way to a mandate for accountability. Rather than assessing costs and building a fee for service, the not-for-profit information agency works within the parameters of a known budget. Consequently, the manager must carefully determine cost/benefit ratios relative to customer need and demand, in order to make product decisions that are grounded in the tenets of accountability to funding authorities and/or taxpayers. The "bottom line" is not cost recovery; rather, it is stewardship.

Several variables come into play as that stewardship is examined. First, the service ethic has matured through many decades of evolving librarianship. This service ethic has fostered attitudes of trying to be all things to all people, of dealing with "patrons" on a one-to-one basis, of trying to "go the extra mile" in order to satisfy a "patron" request. As noteworthy as this ideal is, in some ways the service ethic operates as an antithesis to effective management, for the attempt to satisfy everyone—particularly in a time of economic constraint—often results in diminished products.

However, even in those libraries/information agencies in which the service ethos is strong, some staff members continue to prefer the term "patron" and shy away from using the word "customer." This is the second variable, which denotes the type of relationship that is in place between producer and consumer. Because language is a reflection of thought and attitude, the choice of terms is significant. The word "patron" is associated with the act of giving support and protection, whereas "customer" implies payment for a product or service and is a better reflection of what is actually transpiring.[1]

A third variable follows in step with the service ethic: the continual effort to foster goodwill. In order to be all things to all people, the agency feels compelled to engender an atmosphere of goodwill that is all-inclusive of every public contact. While a worthy goal, the perpetual quest for absolute goodwill can be exhausting. As with all virtues, a tempering of even worthy goals to mesh comfortably with institutional priorities is essential to effective management and responsive product development.

A fourth variable, the expenditure of the tax dollar, is tied to a multitude of process elements. The overall budget has an umbrella effect upon product development and enters every phase of the decision-making process. Further, those decisions that expend tax dollars have impact both upon product development and upon the resultant accountability. Careful stewardship is not simply a conservative activity; rather, it is the deliberate, informed assessment, based upon the marketing audit, of how, when, and where community needs can be best addressed.

Finally, the act of allocating resources to provide the maximum strength of product in both quality and numbers may well be the ultimate test of good management. Stretching resources has been a quagmire into which many managers have unwittingly strayed. By attempting to continue an existing array of products in the face of declining resources, these managers have plastered a band-aid solution onto a severe economic injury. As long as funding authorities perceive that the agency's products can continue in spite of budget reductions, little incentive exists to make restitution. There are no easy answers, but there are challenges to be faced with good information and good humor.

A UNIQUE PRODUCER:
THE INFORMATION AGENCY

There are many services and programs that might be part of a library/information agency's stable of products (see figure 6.1). The most common element is diversity. A library/information agency's products are necessarily eclectic to meet the needs of a heterogeneous community. Even private or corporate libraries, whose customers have more focused needs, will have the surprising potential for quite a list of products.

Reference/information service
Telephone information service
Interloan
Selective Dissemination of Information (SDI)
Story hours
Programs: puppet shows, film series, tax assistance, etc.
Learner's adviser service
Information and referral
Circulation of materials
Circulation of equipment
Lending of toys, tools, art prints, etc.
Collections of materials: bestsellers, video, films, books,
    magazines, etc.
Homebound service
Access via cable television or computer
Online catalog
CD-ROM database access
Use of audiovisual equipment/computers
Books by mail
Bookmobile service
Study carrels, wet and dry
Meeting rooms
Reserve materials

Fig. 6.1. Information agency products.

It is important to remember that, in any given year, an agency's product decisions should relate to both current or existing products and potential products. Consideration of the entire span of product development (see the section on product life cycle later in this chapter) is essential to both short- and long-range planning— and definitely to marketing as well. Planning teams must be continually assessing the status of different products, with an eye toward historical evolution, current effectiveness, and future potential.

The Product—Circles Within Circles

The <u>concept of product</u> is complex and involves a series of levels and related factors. Philip Kotler has configured the concept of product according to three primary definitions:

1. *Product mix*—the set of all product lines and items that a particular organization makes available to customers.

2. *Product line*—a group of products within a product mix that are closely related, because they function in a similar manner, are made available to the same consumers, or are marketed through the same types of outlets.

3. *Product item*—a distinct unit within a product line that is distinguishable by size, appearance, price, or some other attribute.[2]

Figure 6.2 illustrates the relationship among these three definitions. As an example, if a customer enters a public library seeking a study manual to prepare for a postal service examination, the product item being sought is that manual. The product line in which the manual is found is the entire range of study manuals for various occupations and texts. The product mix would be the total amount of products offered by that public library.

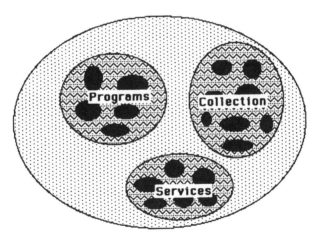

 Product Mix

Product Line

Product Item

Fig. 6.2. Product definitions.

In addition to these three fundamental definitions, Kotler goes on to describe an organization's product mix in three-dimensional terms: length, width, and depth.[3] This dimensional model is depicted in figure 6.3, further demonstrating how the concepts of product mix, product line, and product item interact to form the holistic term: product.

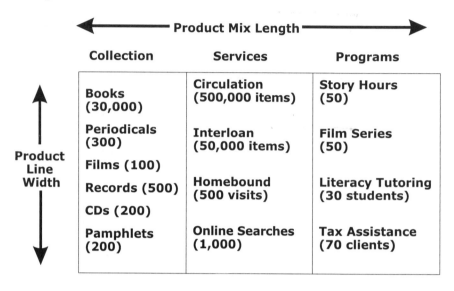

Fig. 6.3. The three-dimensional product mix.

As an example of this model, the product line width might include such items as books, periodicals, films or videos, and audio recordings. The product mix length might incorporate the collection, services, and programs. Finally, since each product item has a certain depth, there may be 30,000 books, 300 periodicals, 100 films, and so forth.

If the information agency were planning to alter this product mix, the following adjustments might occur:

1. *Product mix:* lengthen by adding an in-house restaurant operation; or contract by discontinuing programs (as an illustration only—not recommended).

2. *Product line:* expand by adding another format, such as videos or audio books; or contract by eliminating films.

3. *Product item:* increase depth by increasing the size of the collection; or contract by decreasing collection size through vigorous weeding and little or no replacement.

These examples of expansion and contraction illustrate the inherent complexity, interrelationships, and fluidity of the simple term: product.

Levels of Product Analysis

Kotler further explains "product" by defining the concept as "anything that can be offered to a market to satisfy a need. It includes physical objects, services, persons, places, organizations, and ideas. Other names for a product would be the offer, value package, or benefit bundle."[4] In addition, he expands upon the product concept by distinguishing three levels: the core, tangible, and augmented levels.[5]

Figure 6.4 displays product levels or attributes as an "apple": a core product, a tangible product, and an augmented product. The core product reflects what the customer is really seeking: information, a place to read newspapers and magazines, an opportunity for socialization, and so forth. The core product is generally made available to the customer in some tangible form: books, journals, electronic display, comfortable seating. Finally, the augmented product consists of corollary or additional benefits: use of audiovisual equipment or computers, referral to an additional source, staff friendliness, speed of retrieval, etc.[6]

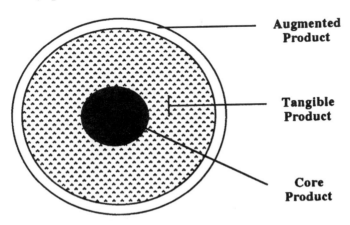

Augmented Product

Tangible Product

Core Product

Fig. 6.4. Product attributes. Adapted from Darlene E. Weingand, *Customer Service Excellence: A Concise Guide for Librarians* (Chicago: American Library Association, 1997), 37.

To further build upon this model: The core product answers the questions What is the consumer really seeking and what need is the product really satisfying? In the example of the customer seeking the study manual for the postal service test, the obvious product is the manual itself, but the true core product is the information present in that manual that will help the customer take the test successfully.

Further, the core product is generally made available to the customer in some tangible form. The tangible product has up to five characteristics: *styling, features, quality level, packaging,* and *brand name.* In the example, the tangible product is the manual itself; its *styling* includes readability, size of type, and ease of use. The *features* of the tangible product include the customer's right to check out the manual and take it home for more convenient study. The *quality level* refers to the currency of the manual and its physical condition. The *packaging* characteristic refers to the larger network within which the public library operates, including the ability to secure the manual via interloan if it is not readily available. Finally, the *brand name* is a section of the library called the "Job Information Center," in which all occupational self-study manuals are located.

The *augmented product* in this example includes the additional services and benefits that go beyond the tangible product, such as referral to supplementary materials or to a tutor, information concerning the date and place of the test, the warm atmosphere of the library, the helpfulness of the staff, and so forth.

It is apparent that the concept of "product" has many facets, and although these multiple aspects of product can be difficult to cost out, both direct and indirect costs can and should be assigned to each product (see chapter 7).

PRODUCT DESIGN

How are products determined? What decisions need to be made in order to develop the most appropriate products? The foundation, as has been stated repeatedly, is the marketing audit. No decision making can be considered reasonable and realistic, much less effective, without a careful assessment of the internal and external environments in which the information agency must operate.

If the foundation is the marketing audit, then the guiding light is the "focus"—keeping the desired position for the information agency always in mind. Focus is the light that illuminates the deliberations of the planning team from the initial discussion of mission, through the setting of goals and objectives, through product design and implementation, and into the creation of promotional strategies. When the planning team is able to focus on the data from the marketing audit and the desired position vis-à-vis the community to be projected, the team's efforts are likely to remain on track.

A Model for Product Analysis

Once all data have been collected and analyzed, both existing target markets and potential new target markets can be identified. A workable model exists, which can serve as an aid in making product decisions relative to target markets. Figure 6.5 demonstrates this two-by-two model.

	Current Products	**Potential Products**
Current Target Markets	**A** **Market Penetration**	**C** **Development of New Products to Meet Needs of Current Market**
Potential Target Markets	**B** **Increase in Number of Target Markets**	**D** **Diversification of Product Line**

Fig. 6.5. The relationship between products and target markets.

Quadrant A illustrates the relationship between current products and current target markets: essentially, a state-of-the-agency condition. This is the arena in which most planning teams generally operate, since the other three quadrants are spin-offs of marketing theories and principles—an uncharted area for many information agencies. Quadrant A represents the traditional, the safe, the familiar. This in no way suggests that Quadrant A should be devalued; the products and target markets that presently exist are vital components of the marketing audit, critical to successful agency operations. The challenge here is to pose ways in which the agency's current product line can be more effectively designed and promoted to further penetrate the existing markets—increase market share. In other words, how can a larger percentage of the present target markets be encouraged to use these products?

As comfortable as it may feel for the planning team to discuss the issues represented in Quadrant A, it is important to note that significant discussions regarding the remaining three quadrants are imperative and should be part of an early planning team agenda.

Quadrant B considers the current products in light of potential target markets other than those presently being served. Discussion would center on strategies for promoting the existing product mix in ways that would directly appeal to these potential market groups. The desired outcome would be an increase in the total number of target markets served by the current product mix.

Quadrant C demonstrates the possibilities that can emerge from consideration of present target markets and the new products that might be developed to better meet their needs. The marketing audit can provide significant insights into the needs of existing markets; creative brainstorming sessions may result in new product ideas that encourage more active use of the agency by the present target markets.

Quadrant D focuses on complete diversification both in target markets and in products. New target markets are sought at the same time that new product development is in the planning stage. This is a true expansion phase for the information agency; the flow of ideas within the organization, synthesized by the planning team, should be nurtured. Creative dynamics can energize the entire organization.

The Relevance of Innovation Theories

The research of Everett Rogers and F. Floyd Shoemaker concluded that, in terms of how quickly people adopt an innovation, the distribution is along a normal bell-shaped curve. Innovators comprise 2.5 percent of the population. Early adopters consist of 13.5 percent, while the early and late majority groups are 34 percent each. Bringing up the rear, laggards appear to be 16 percent.[7]

Further, in Cyril Houle's investigations of researched linkages between rate of adoption of an innovation and continuing education, he discovered that

> a close relationship exists between rate of adoption and each of the following factors: favorable attitude toward education; favorable attitude toward science; extent of contact with people whose function it is to bring about change; amount of exposure to mass media; openness to interpersonal channels of communication; extent of general social participation; cosmopolitanism as contrasted to localism; number of years of formal education; intelligence; and degree of specialization of practice.[8]

How do these theories of innovation relate to product development? If, as Rogers and Shoemaker suggest, the population in any given community can be viewed as being distributed along the bell-shaped curve, then it is incumbent upon the planning team to adjust their time expectations accordingly. A sufficient interval must be built into the planning time line so that the natural process of adoption has the opportunity to take place. In addition, potential clients in each of the depicted groups would require different marketing strategies in order to relate to the information agency's products.

In conjunction with recognition of the innovation curve, it is important that the planning team realize that personal influence can play a critical role in product adoption. Consequently, involving community leaders and popular personalities in product test marketing can be a wise strategy.

Finally, the data collected in the marketing audit should be able to create a community profile that parallels those attributes described by Houle. If the community possesses a large percentage of those traits, the probability of positive adoption of new products is enhanced.

NEW PRODUCT DEVELOPMENT

The process for developing a product mix has seven discrete phases or steps: 1) new product strategy development; 2) idea generation; 3) screening and evaluation; 4) business analysis; 5) product design or development; 6) testing; and 7) commercial introduction. This process is designed to move the product idea along from inception to reality.[9]

The first phase, new product strategy development, integrates well with the goals and objectives components of the planning process. This overall formulation of direction is, of course, an initial stage both of the planning and of the marketing processes.

The second phase, idea generation, is frequently the end result of brainstorming sessions such as those that occur in the Nominal Group process. Following the generation of the maximum number of ideas, a screening process (phase three) is initiated, based upon a business analysis approach (phase four), and assisted by data from the marketing audit.

Table 6.1 can assist the planning team in screening each new product idea. The criteria listed are given assessment values of from one to three points by each member of the team. Horizontal totals are taken to combine the ratings of individual team members on each criterion. The total vertical score can be compared among the various products vying for planning team approval. As current products can also benefit from inclusion in this process, they should be subsequently compared with the final scores of the new product ideas.

Table 6.1. Screening Form for Product Ideas

Product: _____ Date: _____

Description and Use: _____

Major Advantage to Client: _____

Major Disadvantage to Client: _____

CRITERIA	GOOD (3 points)	AVERAGE (2 points)	POOR (1 point)	TOTAL POINTS
1. Information Agency Operations:				
a. Compatible with agency efforts—really our business	___	___	___	___
b. Would not require interruption of present activities	___	___	___	___
c. General know-how available	___	___	___	___
d. Ability to meet client service requirements	___	___	___	___
2. Potential Market:				
a. Market size—volume	___	___	___	___
b. Location	___	___	___	___
c. Market share (potential)	___	___	___	___
d. Diversity—needed by several target markets	___	___	___	___
e. Market growth assured	___	___	___	___
f. Stability in declining budget years	___	___	___	___
g. Foothold in new field	___	___	___	___
3. Marketability:				
a. Estimated price vs. competition	___	___	___	___
b. Have qualified personnel	___	___	___	___
c. Ease of promotability	___	___	___	___
d. Suitability of existing distribution channels	___	___	___	___
e. Originality/differentiation of product	___	___	___	___

CRITERIA	GOOD (3 points)	AVERAGE (2 points)	POOR (1 point)	TOTAL POINTS
3. Marketability: *(continued)*				
f. Degree of competition				
Present				
Potential				
g. Life expectancy of demand				
h. Customer/client loyalty				
i. No opposition from competition				
4. Production:				
a. Feasibility of product				
b. Adequacy of technical capability				
c. Development cost				
d. Adequacy of production capability				
e. Materials availability				
f. Staff availability				
g. Facilities: equipment/space available				
h. Service support available				
i. Storage availability				
5. Budget:				
a. Effective return on investment				
b. Capital availability				
c. Payback period				
TOTAL POINTS (99 maximum)				

Phase five involves the actual product design or development and correlates directly with the parallel formulation of objectives and action strategies. This is the stage in which concrete decisions are made regarding product lines and product items, with the amount of available resources entering into every aspect of the discussion. Priorities established in phases three and four are given a second look in the harsh light of realistic economic and staffing implications.

In addition to consideration of resource opportunities and/or limitations, the planning team may decide to create uniqueness for their products to help achieve a differential advantage in the marketplace. Product differentiation can be achieved through specific product attributes, by creating a distinctive image, by providing unique services, through unique distribution, or by a combination of these tactics.[10] Moreover, the planning team may also wish to consider product positioning and repositioning—focusing marketing strategy efforts toward a particular target market having specific product preferences.[11]

The "short list" that emerges moves on to the next phase: test marketing. Test marketing or pilot projects are mechanisms through which the relationship between proposed products and customer demand can be better ascertained. Figure 7.5 depicts this relationship. However, the planning team should recognize that high cost does not automatically eliminate a product; conversely, low demand does not necessarily mean definite phase out. The ratio between cost and demand that equates to cost/benefit is the ultimate determinant; discussion should center on this aspect of evaluation.

The final phase is the introduction of the product into the product line as a fully integrated item. This implementation may be almost anticlimactic after the range of planning and evaluative activities that preceded it. An important ingredient in the implementation phase is the facilitation of product involvement: the degree to which a product is relevant to a member of a target market and the extent to which the product "speaks" to the client's sense of identity or self-image. Promotional strategies need to be designed to stimulate this involvement and enhance customer response to the product.

THE PRODUCT LIFE CYCLE

Nature has decreed that all life is subject to a cyclical structure: birth, growth, maturation, decline, and death. In the dynamic world of product development, these principles also apply. In other words, the product life cycle is a natural phenomenon and, as such, must be integrated into the thinking of each member of the planning team.

This is not easy. In the for-profit sector, the product life cycle is readily acknowledged. However, in the not-for-profit sector, organizations have difficulty in accepting this concept. The lengthy tradition of attempting to be all things to all people has also left a residue that insists that products go on forever. Information professionals are comfortable and creative when additional monies are available for experimentation and new product development; they are decidedly uncomfortable with the thought that a service must end, a branch must close, or a format must be discontinued. Yet, this terminus is as natural a part of the product life cycle as the creation terminus. It simply is this: Products are generated and introduced, they grow, they mature and are maintained, they decline, and they must eventually be phased out. Figure 6.6 illustrates this progression.

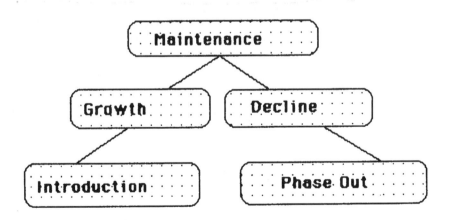

Fig. 6.6. The product life cycle.

Kotler states:

> It is not possible for a product's characteristics and
> marketing approach to remain optimal for all time.
> Broad changes in the macroenvironment (population,
> economy, politics, technology, and culture) as well as
> specific changes in the market environment (buyers,
> competitors, dealers, suppliers) will call for major
> product and marketing adjustments at key points in
> the product's history.[12]

In addition, changes within the library/information agency
(the internal environment) will also play a deciding role in the rate
of product growth and decline.

The planning committee, in its screening analysis of current
and potential products, will be able to monitor the environmental
changes as they occur and the resultant effects upon individual
product items. When the concept of product life cycle is a part of the
planning team's total responsibility, the team can develop marketing mix strategies more effectively to better achieve the information agency's goals and objectives.

Finally, as the totality of the marketing/planning process
has a "bottom line," the bottom line of product development can be
simply stated: *Plan products to satisfy identified needs and wants.*
This basic rule can guide the planning team through all the intricacies
and complexities of effective product development. With this rule in
mind and in practice, the information agency's products will be well
designed and well suited to the identified target markets.

It is difficult, however—if not impossible—to assess product
effectiveness without knowledge of what each product costs to offer
to the community. In the next chapter, the second "P" of marketing,
Price, is added to the marketing mix.

Scenario for Further Thought: Product Design

The Brownton College is situated in a small midwestern town on a campus serving 2,000 students and 300 faculty. Within commuting distance of a large metropolitan area (with a major public library), the town is also fairly close to an extensive rural community (with small public libraries open only ten to twenty hours per week).

The library's planning team is in the midst of product development, is attempting to differentiate between its product mix, product lines, and product items. What would be reasonable inclusions in each of these three categories?

Product Mix

Product Lines

Product Items

NOTES

1.   Darlene E. Weingand, *Customer Service Excellence: A Concise Guide for Librarians* (Chicago: American Library Association, 1997), 2.

2.   Philip Kotler, *Marketing for Nonprofit Organizations,* 2d ed. (Englewood Cliffs, N.J.: Prentice-Hall, 1982), 289.

3.   Ibid., 289–90.

4.   Ibid., 291.

5.   Ibid., 291–96.

6.   Weingand, *Customer Service Excellence,* 37–38.

7.   Everett M. Rogers and F. Floyd Shoemaker, *Communication of Innovations, A Cross Cultural Approach*, 2d ed. (New York: Free Press, 1971), 182.

8.   Cyril O. Houle, "Evidence for the Effectiveness of Continuing Professional Education and the Impact of Mandatory Continuing Education," in *Proceedings: Mandatory Continuing Education: Prospects and Dilemmas for Professionals,* ed. Donald E. Moore, Jr. (Urbana, Ill.: University of Illinois Press, 1976), 124.

9.   Walton Beacham, Richard T. Hise, and Hale N. Tongren, *Beacham's Marketing Reference,* vol. 2 (Washington, D.C.: Research Publishing, 1986), 671.

10.   Ibid., 676.

11.   Ibid., 709.

12.   Kotler, *Marketing for Nonprofit Organizations,* 296.

=== ☙

Chapter 7

The Price—What Does Each Product Cost?

❧ ————————————————————————————————————

The concept of price—or cost—may be the most confusing of all the elements of the marketing mix. The traditional view of library service emerges from the public library heritage and has evolved into a standard of "free" service. In today's world—where local governments are trying to stretch the tax dollar to cover a multiplicity of important services, where academic institutions are turning to distance education to attract more students, where corporations continue to downsize, and where schools struggle to acquire needed technology—this historical concept of library service is under increasing stress. The assumptions of operation are shifting as society attempts to cope with escalating change.

The need to look objectively at the concept of price/cost is critical to any type of information service; the principles can be generalized to include the entire spectrum of information providers. The discipline of identifying costs will assist the library in specifying the expenses related to various program elements and developing program priorities.

WHAT DOES PRICE MEAN?

Although price is given as a mnemonic device, the actual working definition is cost: The cost to produce a product. In the profit sector, the cost to produce an item is straightforward: All cost factors, both direct and indirect, are calculated and a price for the goods or services is set based upon those factors plus a margin of profit. In the nonprofit sector, an inverse approach must be applied: The budget is the known quantity and all possible information services must compete for a share of those dollars. In both sectors, the cost factors are similar; it is the decision-making process that changes.

The "fee versus free" controversy that appears repeatedly in library literature tends to oversimplify the issue of costing. When fiscal concerns become subsumed in such a debate, the very important issues of costing can be easily overlooked. For example, tradition dictates that certain basic library products (such as collection, reference, story hours, etc.) must always be considered "free," whereas newer products (such as videos, rental collections, or on-line searching) may have a fee assigned. Rather than using the marketing/planning process to identify customer needs and designing products to meet those needs, products become categorized into what is "free" and what could possibly generate revenue.

Although historical tradition certainly has an impact, the primary determinant in considering the issue of whether to charge a fee is the organizational mission. A public library may be committed to the concept of "free" service, although we must clearly understand that services are certainly not "free." However, such a library may wish to absorb direct user charges for a certain level of basic service in order to maintain equity of user access, but charge variable fees for service of more depth or duration. Public library boards of trustees serve as policymakers, and increasing numbers of municipalities are seeking to influence these policy decisions.

Academic and school libraries, which operate under specific institutional missions, may need to run fee proposals through designated bureaucratic channels before implementing. Special libraries, too, will have an internal organizational structure to negotiate before instituting or changing policies. Entrepreneurial information agencies in business to make a profit, however, find no ethical or historical barriers to confront. Operating as any for-profit business, these agencies will assign a cost/price ratio accordingly.

Assuming for purposes of discussion that a fee structure is desired for a given product or products, several questions must be considered before putting policy into practice:

1. If a fee is assigned, what will be the effect in terms of community support? (Community here is defined as constituency groups or target markets.) If the cost of instituting a fee is loss of community support for the agency, then that cost may well be too high in relationship to potential monetary gain. It is imperative that the marketing audit look at this concern and provide data so that an informed decision can be made.

2. What shall the fee be? There are two types of pricing tactics: *price taking* is the assignment of a fee that matches the going rate, that is, what is being charged by other agencies in similar situations; *price making* is the setting of a fee based on the position the agency desires in the marketplace. The first is reactive; the second is proactive. The decision once again is based on the agency mission and goals plus the information secured in the marketing audit. The process of structuring a long-range plan, a marketing audit, and a focused marketing/planning process will reveal the type of pricing strategies needed to carry out the plan.[1]

3. What is the purpose of the fee? An apparent purpose is profit, but whether that profit would be free and clear or a mechanism to reduce demand on regular budget monies is an important decision. Again, this decision is tied to agency mission and goals.

Questions such as these are important to answer well in advance of any action. One of the imperatives for decision making within the context of a marketing/planning process is the consideration of all contingencies and alternatives. Management is then able to make informed decisions based on the best possible present and projected information.

As one of the key elements in the marketing plan, price seeks out all present and potential cost factors. These factors include direct costs, indirect costs, personnel costs, profit (if applicable), and intangibles. All of these factors are incorporated into the information agency's budget. Careful analysis of these various factors results in a realistic appraisal of what a product actually costs to produce and serves as input in the decision of whether or not to produce it. In other words, knowing the projected cost figures provides a benchmark against which demand factors can be compared. (The cost versus demand relationship is further discussed later in this chapter.) Such an assessment, when measured against the library's goals and objectives, helps the library determine service priorities that are practical, yet in tune with its mission.

COSTING AND BUDGETING

There is a direct relationship between cost factors and the budgeting process. The decision-making process required to allocate limited dollars can be frustrating and time-consuming, particularly when adequate information is not available. To make informed budget decisions, the identification of all cost factors is essential. The "bottom line" here is a simple question: What does each product contribute to the information agency? In order to be viable, a product must advance the agency toward its goals and be consonant with its stated mission. In order to assess the level of contribution and the most effective strategies for conducting such an assessment, several aspects need to be considered.

The Program Budget

Many types of budget formats can be used. Municipalities and institutions frequently have definite requirements concerning the format to be submitted. Such conformity is understandable from the funding authority's point of view because it makes the task of comparison of budget requests from multiple units an easier exercise. However, the standard format, which is commonly the *line item budget*, may be less effective from the information agency's planning perspective. Whatever the official requirement, developing *a program budget* meshes logically with the process of identifying cost factors for each library product. (Note: The term *program budget* is popularly used. However, "program" and "product" should be viewed as synonymous.) Figure 7.1 illustrates a simplified program budget.

Program budgeting allows the total agency budget to be constructed program by program. By allocating all debits and credits to individual products, it becomes a relatively simple matter to defend a budget in like manner: program by program. Whereas it is a rather clinical, objective exercise for a funding authority to mandate a 3 percent cut in an overall budget, or perhaps in a particular budget category, it is much more graphic—and difficult—to face the possible elimination of a well-recognized, effective program.

Example of a Line Item Budget	
Direct Costs	
Personnel	$20,000[12]
Supplies	1,600[13]
Materials	22,500[14]
Equipment	8,500[15]
Indirect Costs	8,000[16]
Total Budget	**$60,600**[17]

[12] - The sum of all personnel costs in the program budget
[13] - The sum of all supplies expenses in the program budget
[14] - The sum of all materials expenses in the program budget
[15] - The sum of all equipment costs in the program budget
[16] - The sum of all indirect costs in the program budget
[17] - Equal to the sum of totals of each program

Example of a Program Budget			
Budget Category	**Product 1: Reference Service**	**Product 2: Audio Books**	**Product 3: Story Hours**
Direct Costs			
Personnel	$10,000	$ 5,000	$5,000
Supplies	1,000[2]	200[3]	400[4]
Materials	10,000[5]	10,000[6]	2,500[7]
Equipment	5,000[8]	3,000[9]	500[10]
Indirect Costs [11]	5,000	2,000	1,000
Subtotals	$31,000	$20,200	$9,400

Total Budget: $60,600

[1] - [This information is extremely simplified, and the numeric values given are simply for purposes of illustration. These budgets are adapted from those presented in Darlene E. Weingand, *Managing Today's Public Library: Blueprint for Change* (Englewood, CO: Libraries Unlimited, Inc., 1994), 139–140.]
[2] - Computer paper, computer disks, signage, etc.
[3] - Signage, promotional flyers, etc.
[4] - Craft materials, puppets, etc.
[5] - Reference books, CD-ROM subscriptions, etc.
[6] - Cost of purchasing audio books
[7] - Picture books purchased for use in story hours
[8] - Computer, printer, CD-ROM
[9] - Cassette deck, headphones
[10] - Puppet stage
[11] - Heat, light, rent, janitorial, etc.

Fig. 7.1. Budget examples. Adapted from Darlene E. Weingand, "What Do Products/Services Cost? How Do We Know?" *Library Trends* 43, no. 3 (Winter 1995), 404.

Therefore, it may be to the library's advantage to prepare two budgets: the required version for the funding authority and an operational program budget for the library itself. This is not a difficult task, since the totals from a series of program budgets can be easily summed and placed into the broader categories required by a line item format or other type of structure. In addition, the presentation of a final budget to a funding authority can be considerably enhanced if the details of a program-based budget are available as supporting documentation.

Fixed and Variable Costs

In the development of any product/service, certain costs must be consigned to the fixed category, remaining unchanged despite wide fluctuations in an activity. Building costs are fixed, as they do not change in relation to the level of the library's activity. Variable costs, however, change directly in proportion to fluctuations in an activity. Salaries, material, and online costs are examples of variable costs because they change in relation to such factors as the amount of time worked or number of searches performed.[2] Fixed costs need to be calculated carefully as there is little flexibility; variable costs can serve as a buffer for the total budget outlay for a particular product.

Impact

Assessment of the contribution of a given product is closely tied to its impact on the target market. To determine impact, data must be collected before and after installation of a new product. This data collection, an essential element in the evaluation process, should be viewed as a necessary tool rather than an undesirable or unnecessary activity. Data may be quantitative, such as that gathered by survey, and/or qualitative, such as human interest anecdotal evidence gathered from interviews. Proven impact is probably one of the most influential components in a budget presentation and should be regarded with respect.

Cost/Benefit Analysis

Calculating costs in isolation without investigating the consequences or benefits that a present or proposed product might bring to the customer is of marginal usefulness. For example, a product might appear to be quite reasonable to produce and yet be only minimally effective if customer convenience is not considered. Cost-benefit analysis examines the full range of cost factors for an existing or proposed product (including fixed and variable, direct and indirect), plus those intangible factors such as time and convenience. (Figure 7.2 presents examples of categories of cost factors.) Then it goes further by identifying present and potential benefits of that product to the library's customers. These two sides of the equation—cost and benefit—are determined for each present and proposed product so that a thorough analysis of product feasibility can be made.[3]

Library Costs	Customer Costs	Intangible Costs
Cost to purchase the material Staff cost required to acquire and process the material Indirect costs associated with the operation of the library Delivering the material to the customer (if applicable)	Time, cost and trouble to physically go to the library, or connect electronically Anxiety over when— or if—the material can be secured Wait until the material is available or arrives	Speed Convenience Timeliness Accuracy Staff attitude

Fig. 7.2. Costs involved in connecting customers with products. Adapted from Darlene E. Weingand, "What Do Products/Services Cost? How Do We Know?" *Library Trends* 43, no. 3 (Winter 1995), 404.

The ratio to be derived from analyzing the expenses, revenues (if any), and benefits of the installation of a product is critical in the determination of pricing strategy. It is the process by which the product's contribution is related to customer service and the total agency picture. The decisions involved in allocating the information agency's finite number of dollars should be correlated to the identification of those products with the most favorable ratio between costs and benefits. Working through this process eliminates the "decision-in-a-vacuum" syndrome that can be all too prevalent in administrative decision making.

Direct and Indirect Costs

Direct costs are those items that can be attributed to specific products, whereas indirect costs cover elements that relate to the library's total operations. Direct costs are the easiest costs to identify because they involve an immediate or encumbered expenditure. Other cost categories are less obvious, but are important components of the entire pricing strategy.

The three other components of the 4 Ps must be considered along with the pricing component when considering direct costs. The first P—*product*—and its production amass a large portion of the direct costs. These expenses include those costs entailed in the actual producing or purchasing activities, such as equipment, raw materials, postage, and so forth. The next P—*place*—incurs such costs as rental, interior decoration, and rewiring. For the last P—*promotion*—dollars are spent for advertising, printing, postage, and related costs. While there are personnel costs to be aware of in all three of these corollary categories, these costs should be clustered together as a personnel direct cost item.

Indirect costs are difficult to assign to individual products because they cross over several (or all) products. These costs reflect what might otherwise be viewed as operational expenses. Figure 7.3 gives examples of both direct and indirect costs and illustrates how such categories as personnel and supplies can appear as both direct and indirect cost items.

Direct Costs	Indirect Costs
Rental of space and/or equipment	Operation of buildings and equipment, such as rent, heat, light, maintenance, and depreciation
Salaries of personnel hired to work only in conjunction with a particular product	Salaries of permanent library personnel
Additional supplies purchased in support of that product	Supplies from existing stores normally kept in stock
Product-specific services, such as special printing, postage, and so forth	Supplemental services, such as municipal purchasing, billing, printing, and so forth

Fig. 7.3. Examples of direct and indirect costs. Adapted from Darlene E. Weingand, *Managing Today's Public Library: Blueprint for Change* (Englewood, Colo.: Libraries Unlimited, 1994), 137.

Personnel

Personnel that must be hired for a specific product implementation, over and above the regular staff, should be regarded as a direct cost. These special staff members may include full- or part-time people and volunteers who are added temporarily to the permanent staff. Also included in this category are those individuals or companies whose services are secured via contract.

In terms of indirect personnel costs, it is all too easy to overlook permanent staff members because they are part of every product produced by the agency. However, it is just this intrinsic involvement that mandates that permanent staff time be parceled out among the various programs and services. Accomplishing this end is tricky, but not impossible. There are two assumptions that must be recognized: 1) permanent staff time is involved in every product/service and 2) both wages and fringe benefits must be assessed and incorporated into the calculations.

Supplies

Every agency carries a normal operational supplies allocation. These supplies are included in the indirect cost calculations. However, when supplies are purchased specifically for a product/service implementation, which are above and beyond the supplies maintained for normal administrative operations, they must be considered part of the direct costs.

While indirect costs can be somewhat difficult to apportion to various products, a formula may be used that is based upon the distribution of staff time. The most widely used mechanism for apportioning time is the daily log. The daily log does not need to be an excessive burden upon the staff. If a form is created whereby the staff member simply enters a periodic check mark by the product being worked on, little effort is expended upon additional record keeping. (For a sample staff time log, see figure 7.4.) For maximum efficiency and computer application either now or in the future, the form should be created or adapted so that it can easily be entered into a data processing system.

Once the form is developed and issued to the staff, a sample of days should be selected during which this log will be kept. This sample can be a continuous time slot, such as two weeks, or a random sample of days throughout a specified time period. Selection of the sample frame will depend upon each agency's individual situation and the nature of the products that it handles. Advice and expertise concerning sampling and data collection are frequently available through the business or statistics departments of local high schools, colleges, universities, or technical schools. Local businesses may also have personnel who can be of assistance.

Date:

Staff Member:

COLLECTION

Books														
Periodicals														
Films														
Records														
CD's														
Pamphlets														
etc.														

SERVICES

Circulation														
ILL														
Homebound														
Online														
etc.														

PROGRAMS

Story Hours														
Film Series														
Literacy														
Tax Assist														
etc.														

Fig. 7.4. Sample time log.

When staff personnel cost percentages have been determined and apportioned, based on the data gathered in the time log, similar percentages can be applied to indirect costs. The amount of time percentages allocated to indirect expenses should correlate approximately to the percentage of hours expended by permanent staff on any given product/service. Whether this "quick and dirty" allocation of indirect costs is selected or a more complex model is selected (such as Philip Rosenberg's *Cost Finding for Public Libraries*[4]), it is important to include indirect as well as direct costs when determining pricing strategy.

Intangibles—The Subjective Factors

Subjective factors are elusive and difficult to grasp, but essential in terms of pricing strategy. In information services, such factors include customer convenience, speed, and accuracy. These elements, critical components of an excellent product (see chapter 6), have real pricing implications. They can be relative to personnel expertise, equipment quality, number of database subscriptions, quality of the collection, access issues, and so forth. All of these variables have impact on the agency budget and costing structure. Hard decisions must be made in terms of trade-off: For example, how much speed is the agency willing to sacrifice by virtue of buying a less expensive modem? How do electronic connections and hours of operation affect customer convenience?

Another set of intangibles is frequently defined in the profit sector as "loss leaders" and "bread and butter" services. Loss leaders are those products offered below cost to intrigue a potential customer. Bread and butter services are those products so basic to the operation of the organization that they are considered core services. In information agencies, this set of intangibles could be approached in two very different ways:

1. The loss leaders are the bread and butter services; that is, putting the lowest possible fee (or free) structure on basic services in order to stimulate consumer use of other products. (*Example:* Free use of the video collection in order to promote other agency services.)

2. A supplementary product is designated the loss leader in order to stimulate use of bread and butter services. (*Example:* A library provides Internet access for the community in order to encourage use of its other products.)

The intangibles, introduced in chapter 6 as the "augmented product," respond to attitudinal concerns of the target market groups. They have the potential to "make or break" a product in the eyes of the customer.

SETTING SERVICE PRIORITIES: COST VERSUS DEMAND

One of the key outcomes of the marketing audit is the projection of anticipated demand for each present and potential product. Demand must then be weighed against the identified cost factors. An entire series of questions relates to anticipated demand:

- *What is the competition?*
  Is there duplication of this product by some other agency or group?
  If so, can my agency do it better or for less cost?
  Is there potential for growth in the target market so that more than one provider of this product is reasonable?
  Should we provide this product?

- *What is the involvement of the target market?*
  How important is this product to the target market right now?
  Is there a preexisting relationship between the target market and the product?

- *How complex are the information-gathering and decision-making processes?*
  Are agency resources available to undertake this analysis of market relationship to product (assuming that this analysis is beyond the capability of the marketing audit)?

This ratio of cost to demand determines the viability of a product in relation to all other potential services and to the known agency budget. An extremely cost-effective product/service with little demand is not truly cost-effective. A high-cost product with great demand may well be cost-effective. Figure 7.5 illustrates the relationship between cost and demand.

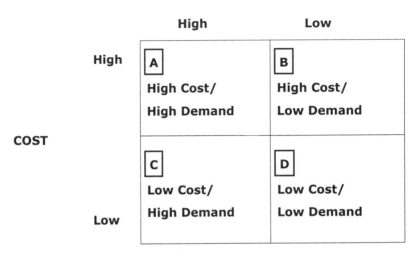

DEMAND

	High	Low
High	**A** High Cost/ High Demand	**B** High Cost/ Low Demand
Low	**C** Low Cost/ High Demand	**D** Low Cost/ Low Demand

COST

Fig. 7.5. The relationship between proposed products and consumer demand.

Quadrant A = products having a high demand, but also requiring a high level of cost to produce.

Quadrant B = products with low demand, but having a corresponding high cost.

Quadrant C = products with low cost implications, but generating high demand.

Quadrant D = products with both low demand and low cost.

Once all costs have been identified, every product offered by the library/information agency should be assigned to one of the four quadrants. Quadrant A products require a decision-making process, as they are both expensive and popular. Quadrant D is also a difficult call, because these products are inexpensive to produce but demand is also low. Quadrant C, however, is every manager's dream: products that cost little but are well regarded by customers. And finally, Quadrant B products should be destined for downsizing or elimination because they are expensive and command little customer interest.

Cost and demand are important ingredients to be considered when service priorities are to be established. However, other factors are also relevant. At the beginning of this chapter, the difference between decision making in the profit and not-for-profit sectors was briefly discussed. To review, in the profit sector, all cost factors are calculated and the price is set accordingly. In the not-for-profit sector, every product competes for a share of the known budget dollar, unless the decision has been made to seek supplemental funding. This essential difference in approach that must be acknowledged at the outset will vary from agency to agency depending upon the institutional affiliation. It will have important effects upon the setting of service priorities.

A second major influence upon priority setting is the agency's relationship to its target markets. If representatives of these target markets have been included on the planning committee so that their needs are continually monitored—and if an effective pattern of communication is maintained—then the information gathered, particularly in terms of needs and demand, will be invaluable in the process of setting service priorities.

Another relationship to be considered is that between priorities and the objectives and action strategies of the planning process. Service priorities must not only respond to mission and target markets, but also to the goals of the agency, with attendant objectives and actions. If all these planning elements are added to the mix, the setting of priorities becomes not only less nebulous, but also less tedious. There is real data to serve as the basis for decision making; there is knowledge about cost, demand, impact, and customers that brings meaning and validity to the entire process.

Price is indeed a difficult element in the marketing mix; however, its importance must be acknowledged. Its presence adds the dimension of practicality that is so critical to informed decision making. Pricing considerations affect product development, distribution, and promotion. There is simply no operating without attention to price; it is the structure that supports the other elements of the marketing mix.

Scenario for Further Thought: Price/Cost

1. The Alpha Information Service is a new small business about to enter into the information market in a small midwestern city of 50,000 people. The city has a public library. Alpha's two owners have experience in library science and computer searching, but little background in business. What should these owners do relative to price to assure the best possible start? Rank in terms of priorities:

   - Take accounting courses
   - Contact the Small Business Administration
   - Do a marketing audit
   - Study the competition
   - Identify their costs
   - Start a planning process
   - Investigate possible demand
   - Do marketing research
   - Practice their searching skills
   - Contact the public library
   - Advertise in the newspaper
   - Other???

2. Alpha Public Library operates in the same city. How could/should the library respond to this new, competing business? How would the library's pricing strategy be affected?

NOTES

1. Judith B. Ross, "New Strategies: Price and the Behavioral Learning Model," in *Marketing Public Library Services: New Strategies,* comp. Darlene E. Weingand (Chicago: American Library Association, 1985), 59.

2. Herbert Snyder, "Allocating Costs: Is It a Program Worth Keeping?" *Library Administration & Management* 12, no. 3 (Summer 1998), 167.

3. Darlene E. Weingand, *Future-Driven Library Marketing* (Chicago: American Library Association, 1998), 100–101.

4. Philip Rosenberg, *Cost Finding for Public Libraries: A Manager's Handbook* (Chicago: American Library Association, 1985).

Chapter 8

═══════════════════════════════════ ○ℬ

The Place—How to Connect the Customer with the Product

℘○ ─────────────────────────────────

The word *place* is relatively clear when the product is secured at a single location. The concept becomes more complex when multiple sites are involved or when the full range of distribution possibilities (including electronic) is applied. To understand the implications of this element of the marketing mix, it is necessary to approach the concept from a definitional perspective, examining *place* in the context of product distribution and the decisions that ultimately must be made. For the purposes of this discussion, *place* is considered synonymous with *distribution.*

DESIGNING THE CHANNELS OF DISTRIBUTION

Distribution, in its most basic definition, is the *channel* that links the product and the customer. Clearly, there must be some mechanism provided so that this connection may take place. A product that is located in one physical site and a customer who is at a different location must at some point come together if an interaction is to occur. However, distribution, as a component of the marketing mix, does not exist as a solo entity. There are definite relationships to be acknowledged.

Relationship to the
Marketing Audit

The baseline for all distribution decisions is the marketing audit. Marketing principles dictate that customer needs and wants should drive the ranking of service priorities, including the distribution decisions. The marketing audit provides a clear picture of what those needs and wants are, both today and into the near future. Effective decision making simply cannot take place without an analysis of customer needs, locational pattern of customers, areas of service delivery, duplication and competition in the market, and recommendations for service alterations. This data will determine the nature of the product, its format, and the relative speed with which the product should/could be delivered. The audit also identifies existing distribution channels, providing input for decisions regarding potential channels: the information so critical to creating distribution channels that operate in everyone's best interest.

Several distribution alternatives exist, each with potential channels (somewhat analogous to a tree effect); these alternatives concern type, number, and location of potential channels. In libraries, distribution alternatives occur on a variety of levels: 1) request for and dissemination of information; 2) programmatic activities; 3) user browsing; and 4) cooperation with corollary agencies. Each of these levels may have various channels of distribution, whether through physical locations or electronic delivery systems. Therefore, a "tree" effect might be envisioned as the library extends "branches" of distribution toward the needs of its customers. Figure 8.1 depicts this concept.

The possibilities can, of course, be extended. What is important to remember is that these alternatives can—and should—be identified for any product before final decisions are made. The marketing audit is the primary source to secure data for constructing these alternatives. Coordination of administration and service with the multiple levels of potential interface is a challenging task, but one with which managers must be proficient if customers are to be provided with the best possible service.

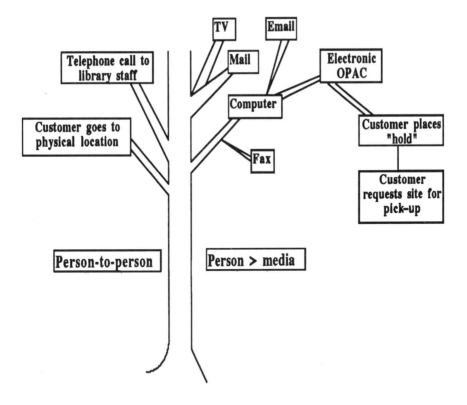

Fig. 8.1. The "tree" concept of distribution.

Relationship to Planning
Elements and the 4 Ps

First, the product itself must be of good quality. Product excellence must be the foundation of the marketing effort, as even an unlimited supply of clever strategies will fail if the product itself is not worthy of customer usage. Further, each product has a finite life cycle (see chapter 6), which is deeply affected by societal change and technological development. Consequently, product evaluation must be directed not only to quality, but also to pricing and distribution. It is not unreasonable to project that a product's life expectancy might be considerably extended if the method of distribution were modified to more closely correlate with the needs of a changing society. For example, a public library story hour operating in an area where the preschool population is declining significantly might be designed in cooperation with local daycare centers and/or produced on local access cable television.

Once quality is assured, it is necessary to consider price. Is the price of producing this product equitable for both the agency and customer? Have all product costs been calculated and apportioned? Has the cost/benefit ratio been determined? Has the anticipated demand been verified? Finally, have service priorities been established?

When these questions have been answered to the information agency's satisfaction, it is then time to address the strategies of distribution in the light of future promotion. To be successful, promotional efforts must focus on the communication of benefits to customers. Some of those benefits should include the distribution channels that have been created. With the goal of customer needs and benefits in mind, under the guidance of the agency mission and goals, distribution channels can be designed to effectively link all 4 Ps together into a well-conceived marketing plan.

In addition, the agency mission statement, together with the goals and objectives formulated in the marketing/planning process, determines the answers to the following crucial questions:

- What shall be the level and quality of service?

- Who are the target markets?

- Who shall pay the relative costs of distribution?

These questions must be carefully considered before any distribution decisions are attempted. The answers may be deeply affected by current economic conditions, and may also be influenced by legislative actions. Whereas the decades of the 1960s and 1970s were expansive with governmental monies and services, the subsequent decades of the 1980s and 1990s saw retrenchment and downsizing, often resulting in a reordering of agency priorities. Accountability has become a major yardstick for funding authorities, and library/information agency managers have been required to stretch budget dollars while still offering effective products. Cooperative ventures are seen as a remedy for duplication of services. In such an environment, distribution becomes more than customer convenience; it is the issue of access, and equity of access becomes more prominent in times of economic constraints.

Both convenience and access are affected by the costs of distribution. The relationship between actual dollar costs and maximum consumer convenience is a teeter-totter upon which the information agency and the customer are perched. Dollar costs include costs of production of the product/service and the customer costs of reaching that product (such as transportation or telecommunication expense). In addition to customer dollar costs, the costs of time and inconvenience must be calculated. The sum of these costs might be directly equated to access—whether the customer really has (or can afford) access to the desired product(s).

The problems and opportunities of distribution demand creative thinking and a willingness to take risks. There will be a whole spectrum of solutions to distribution problems, many less than optimal. If the planning and marketing elements are correlated into a unified plan, it will be easier to identify options. It is a marriage of processes that produces the soundest structure for successful operations.

DISTRIBUTION DECISION FACTORS

In the consideration of distribution possibilities, it is important to remember that the product is removed not only in space from the location of the customer, but may also be removed in time from when the customer wishes to use it. The very real issue of the customer's access to the product must be analyzed in broad terms, including both space and time as parameters of concern.

The many decisions made in this dimension of the marketing effort will determine how the product/service will be accessible to the target markets. Effective methods of distribution add value to the product, making it available at convenient times and places. The philosophy of service has great impact here; will distribution be handled in traditional ways, as it has been in the past? Or is the information agency willing to expand its options by using new technologies? Another important issue is that of known distribution problems. Who will bear the costs of solving these problems: the information agency, the customer, or both? All of these questions must be considered.

Nine decision factors (see figure 8.2) are concerned with the distribution flow from initial product determinations through the entire life cycle of the product. Because all nine factors influence decisions, they need to be part of the continuing discussion and evaluation process.

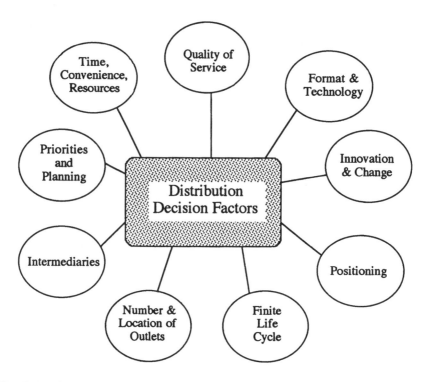

Fig. 8.2. Distribution decision factors.

Quality of Service

Information agencies provide a product based on service, hence the frequent juxtaposition of product/service in this book. However, the information product/service is two-pronged; it is both a product in the ordinary sense, plus it is delivery as well. For information agencies, distribution becomes more than an equal component of the marketing mix: It is also an integral part of the product. As a result, distribution decisions have a pronounced effect upon the product's viability.

Quality wears many faces. Certainly, if library materials are in need of repair, are no longer current, or contain incorrect information, they do not meet even a mediocre standard of quality. Further, information may be less easily verified, but the importance of accuracy and reliability is essential. Therefore, the intrinsic worth of the physical information product or the informational response carries considerable weight in assessing quality.[1]

Yet, there is more to quality than matching the internal quality of tangible and/or intangible information packages to a high standard. William A. Band, in his book, *Creating Value for Customers*, looks at quality through five different lenses, each addressing a different aspect of quality:

- *Transcendent quality:* An innate beauty and excellence as the means to customer satisfaction

- *Product-based quality:* Quality that is measurable and to a high standard; customer satisfaction is achieved by having more of some element or attribute

- *User-based quality:* Only the customer can be the judge of what quality is; users' perceptions of how well their wants and needs are met

- *Operations-based quality:* How closely the product meets the specifications set for it (either by the information agency or by the customer)

- *Value-based quality:* Conformance to requirements, including price and cost of production; meeting customer needs at a competitive price[2]

These lenses are quite different, yet also share common elements. Within any information agency, various staff members will relate more strongly to one or more lenses while other staff members may choose differently. It is necessary to search for the commonalties and to build a definition of quality that can be mutually agreed upon.

Time, Convenience, and Resource Allocation

In addition to intrinsic quality, the attributes of time, convenience, and resource allocation have a significant impact on overall quality. Although speed of access, as an element of time, is normally a first concern, the combination of time and distance must also be considered. In today's world, the customer is bombarded by literally thousands of sensory messages and personal time demands in any given day. Consequently, the less time required to secure needed information will equate to a higher level of service and satisfaction. This customer perception is a critical one: An excellent product must be *perceived* as excellent to achieve that status in real terms.

How can time then be defined?

1. *As the time expended by staff in the process of providing information.* This is the time that occurs from the point of the initial question to the point of the completed response. This portion of the time factor can be controlled through a proper maintenance and deployment of staff and collection resources.

2. *As the time expended in overcoming physical distance between customer and service.* This time component is directly dependent upon distribution decisions. Overcoming of physical distance may be addressed through judicious placement of actual outlets and through creative use of technological delivery systems. There is a great deal of flexibility for the information agency in confronting this portion of time expenditure.

3. *As the real time that service is available to the client.* Whereas the other definitions of time have variables that can be readily controlled through decisions affecting use of tangible resources, this time component relates directly to clock hours. How many hours per day is the service available? How do those hours correlate with the hours that the customer has available? For example, is the service available to a customer who works from midnight to 8:00 A.M.? Or will that person be required to use nonwork time to satisfy his or her work-related information needs? Is this equitable? If, indeed, information is a personal, community, and national resource, should access not serve a twenty-four-hour day? These are very real distribution questions.

The constraints imposed by the three time definitions, including distance as a component of the second definition, can be controlled through the use of innovative distribution channels. Many of the messages and demands that affect a customer's life are precipitated by technological developments, such as mass media or e-mail. It makes sense, then, to consider these same technologies as potential solutions to the problems they have created.

The result of making customer need the driving force will be a variation in the service provided by different outlets or channels. New technologies will enable this variation to take place. Using the public library as an example, the days of requiring branch libraries to contain only those materials that are available in regional and/or main libraries are over; integrated online catalogs and circulation systems allow a flexibility that was not possible in the recent past.

Each distribution channel, whether it be via telecommunications or physical site, can be tailored to specifically meet the needs of the identified target market(s). Design of this nature effectively addresses the issues of time, convenience, and resource allocation.

Priorities and Planning

It is relatively easy to state that customer need should drive the setting of priorities, but much more difficult to accomplish that end. However, when a merged marketing/planning process is developed and implemented, priority setting in the context of customer need becomes a reasonable activity. Annual establishment of an operational plan for the coming year, updating of the five-year long-range plan, and an ongoing marketing effort become the basic framework within which innovative planning and marketing strategies are created.

An important concept to consider when developing the marketing/planning effort is that of "stakeholder management." Peter Davis examines an approach to planned change that looks at perceived barriers to self-initiated planning and proposes strategic efforts to redefine the relationship between the information agency and its environment.[3] In this proactive approach, Davis reaffirms that "stakeholder planning emphasizes strategic participation of those groups who have an important stake in the institution, and who are willing to search for jointly advantageous solutions to problems."[4]

Stakeholder management consists of four features:

1. An approach to planned change.

2. Examination of perceived barriers to self-initiated planning.

3. Proposal of strategic efforts to redefine the relationship between the information agency and its environment.

4. Participation of groups having a stake in the outcome.

One strategy for implementing stakeholder management is through the use of a planning committee composed of representatives of the agency's various constituency groups, plus internal organizational representatives (see chapter 2). In many ways, working with such a planning committee is analogous to having an ongoing marketing audit: The continuous communication linkages and input of data can help to closely monitor the pulse of the community served. In addition, customers are directly involved in structuring the response to their needs, thus fulfilling the model of customer-oriented marketing.

Davis further stresses that "for most libraries the (economic) buffer has gone. The library is closely 'engaged' with its environment and must adapt itself to it. The days in which a library could move into the future riding on past traditions, buffered by a cushion of slack resources, are over."[5]

This latter statement is a testimonial for the relevance of combining the planning and marketing processes so that the information agency truly becomes "engaged" with its environment.

Human Resource Intermediaries

Although the traditional model of service has been structured on a one-to-one interaction between information specialist and customer, today's complex world with its expanding sources of information dictates that a more flexible model be used. In the business world, intermediaries in the sales process are termed "middlemen"; they were introduced into the process because they reduce organizational costs, thus increasing operating efficiency. Middlemen are expert in specific aspects of the movement of the product between the manufacturer and the consumer.

The library profession is not unfamiliar with the concept of middlemen. The terminology is different—most are called "vendors" or "jobbers" and act as intermediaries in the materials ordering process. The expansion of information delivery presents additional opportunities for the creative use of intermediaries. For example, cable television operators can be important in developing linkages between information agencies and individual homes and/or offices; computer system operators (sysops) can perform similar functions with computer networking; shopping mall managers can become the conduit to establish minidistribution points in the ever-increasing number of malls.

Another example is the use of experts in various needed agency functions, such as marketing, financing, fundraising, delivery, technology—this list is only as long or as short as one's imagination! Many opportunities exist for improved service through the use of human intermediaries. These opportunities include: 1) cooperation with corollary human service and governmental agencies regarding joint programs, information and referral, and sharing of physical resources; 2) contractual agreements (sometimes termed "outsourcing") with other service brokers, such as private information entrepreneurs or central cataloging operations, to provide those specific functions to which the agency may be unwilling or unable to commit existing staff; and 3) a development of a dynamic volunteer program to provide service to those customers physically unable (due to disability or age) to contact an existing service outlet.[6] These may not be startling ideas, certainly not as exciting as launching a new technology, but they are potential avenues to better service. Manipulation of the marketing/planning effort to include the widest variety of options is challenging and definitely worth considering.

User Convenience: Number and Location of Outlets

Outlets can be *physical sites* such as buildings, branches, kiosks, or offices. (The kiosk can be placed in areas of greatest need and moved to other areas as needs change.) Physical sites may be quite imposing, such as the central facility in large cities or on college campuses, or they may be more modest, such as a special or school library facility. All of these physical types are valid; their implementation should be directly tied to customer use and convenience.

An important consideration in the design of a physical outlet is termed *atmospherics*. Atmospherics includes the ambience of the facility, the colors used in decoration, the quality of lighting, heating/ventilation/cooling (HVAC) considerations, and the physical comfort provided in seating and space arrangement. A visually pleasing facility, perceived by the customer as comfortable and welcoming, has already developed a firm base for customer satisfaction.

A different type of outlet is *product transmittal*. This can be as simple as "books-by-mail" or homebound service, or as technologically sophisticated as information and materials requests via computer or cable television connections. As new technologies develop, the transmittal options will correspondingly increase. As with physical outlets, product transmittal should be designed to maximize customer convenience, and frequently there is more flexibility in a transmittal system than in a series of physical outlets.

How can these outlet decisions be determined? The marketing audit is a critical baseline not only in setting priorities, but also in the examination of existing and potential service outlets. It has been historically difficult not only to close an existing outlet, but also to instill the sense of risk taking necessary to secure funding for creating alternative outlets, such as kiosks or telecommunications systems. The audit can provide the evidence of customer need that may be a catalyst for innovative change.

Customer-oriented marketing and planning strategies frequently smooth the approach to these alternative modes of service delivery. Outlets are, in basic terms, the points of intersection between customer and product. Each outlet should reflect the needs of the market segment it purports to serve. Traditional groupings of customers may no longer be practical in this changing society as technology, career paths, educational backgrounds, personal needs, and shifting political boundaries create new patterns of human growth and interaction. This changing nature of the customer structure suggests that market segmentation—the concentration on subgroups with more homogeneous characteristics than the whole—may be a useful strategy. In the business world, this approach has proved very effective.

Putting such a strategy to work would involve ongoing market research, contact with identified market segments, and the additional step of testing prototype products to determine where and how needs actually can be met.[7] Communication with identified subgroups via targeted newsletters or Web pages is an effective means of contact and data collection, as well as a means of dispensing news concerning prototype product development. The expansion of product delivery systems creates the occasion for analysis and restructuring of the way the information agency relates to its several markets. It is an exciting prospect.

Format and Technological Delivery

In today's rapidly changing world, these two aspects of distribution may well be the most challenging and exciting. The rate of technological development is accelerating so rapidly that new options for distribution are continually emerging. "Blue sky" ideas that were impractical just a short time ago may be entirely within reach at present or the near future. When discussing paradigm shift, Joel Barker, noted futurist, asks, "What today is impossible to do in your business, but, if it could be done, would fundamentally change what you do?"[8] For example, the ability to access library catalogs from home was only a dream a decade ago; today, it is common practice in many areas.

However, technology must not be admired and purchased for its own sake. As with every other distribution decision, the marketing audit must remain the baseline, and delivery decisions must correlate with the organizational mission and goals. In other words, some formats and delivery mechanisms may be appropriate whereas others may not. The decision must be made in the context of the entire marketing/planning process.

For the purposes of this chapter, *format* shall be considered to be media-based software. Format has implications for storage and retrieval of information, and ultimately for customer absorption; the primary reason for connecting customers and information is the use of that information. Individual differences among customers vary widely, therefore it is important to recognize that information may be most useful in a variety of formats. Some people absorb print material most readily; others find audio material more appealing, particularly if a learning disability is involved. Still others are visually oriented and prefer video or other visual images. Because information can be transmitted through all our senses, and learning styles represent a spectrum of individual preferences, information services have a mandate to provide for this variety of customer needs and desires.

Traditional print sources include books, periodicals, microforms, and documents, all those resources with which librarians are so familiar. Computer software must be added to this list, for even though it is also electronic in nature, it is both print and graphics dominant. Voice recognition is certainly adding a new layer of access, but the printed word is likely to remain the focus for the foreseeable future.

Audiovisual sources include the wide range of audio and visual possibilities: phonodiscs (currently staging a comeback), audiocassettes, digital audio tapes (DAT), films, slides, videodiscs, videocassettes, digital video discs (DVD), compact audio discs (CD)—the list seems to grow daily. Because these sources respond to the diversity of learning styles, they are integral to any information service. In addition, both print and audiovisual formats are basic to the storage and retrieval of information. With the merging of the optical disc and the computer, multiple formats can be combined and information retrieved at remarkable speeds.

The optical disc has additional implications for preservation of information and space allocation. Paper is a perishable item, especially if it is not acid-free, but the optical disc is expected to have an extended life span. In addition, it is impervious to many of the environmental and physical forces that damage more traditional materials. Because at least 55,000 frames are available per disc, the present space requirements to house extensive collections of information will shrink markedly in the future. When electronic databases are added to this scenario, it becomes obvious that the information service of the future will require minimal physical space, yet will have access to more information.

Delivery of information may be as traditional as the physical outlets discussed earlier (telephone and mail) or it may take the form of present and developing technologies, such as cable television, computer networks, teleconferencing, broadcasting systems, satellite transmission, FAX, and many combinations and permutations of these modes. These alternative delivery systems offer greater flexibility, with many opportunities for innovation.

Consider a scenario:

> For maximum user convenience, access to information should be available twenty-four hours per day. There are few, if any, libraries that could afford the cost of staffing such a service goal; such access is obviously beyond the realm of reality. But is it? What if the entire notion of library service being directly tied to an open physical site with adequate staff support is temporarily suspended? In its place, insert a new structure:
>
> 1. The physical service outlets are open for direct use during present (or reduced) hours. Typically, this will range between four and twelve hours per day.
>
> 2. As a complement to this direct use model, the local cable television network offers an interactive system whereby citizens can interact with the library's catalog and/or reference service from the comfort of home.
>
> 3. When the library's physical outlets close for the day, the cable (or computer) network remains operative— through the totality of the day—and library staff take turns working "swing shift" hours, serving as resources to the community via the interactive set up. The result, of course, is twenty-four-hour library access through the creation of a new and innovative service mode. Impossible? Not at all.[9]

This scenario is public-library-based, but the concept may be generalized to any type of information service. The critical point is that creative thinking should be encouraged if traditional models are to be reevaluated in the light of customer needs and the risk taken to serve those needs in innovative ways.

Innovation and Change

All other decision factors are elements that coexist within the firmament of innovation and change. The emphasis in this book on those two forces is quite purposeful: The first, innovation, is a response to the second, change. Society spins faster and faster in the midst of an increasing rate of change; it is innovation—the willingness to experiment with alternative ways of thinking, coping, and responding—that can effectively deal with the dynamic impact of change.

In information services, the same approach applies. Individuals, both information professionals and customers, place somewhere on a bell-shaped curve between the extremes of receptivity and resistance to change. It is important for each person to be aware of the point at which his or her personal placement lies; it is also important for the information professional to realize that this curve is part of the normal human condition, being another component of individual differences.

However, the professional who would be proactive in the distribution of information must learn to move personally toward the receptivity extreme. There is a critical need to be flexible, knowledgeable, and a risk taker in the struggle to respond to opportunity. Professional continuing education can be a valuable strategy in the information worker's ongoing effort to be receptive to a changing world. With the information professional caught in the vortex of both change and the channeling of information, it becomes imperative that considerable energy be directed toward acquiring and sustaining personal receptivity.

The Finite Life Cycle

Although the concept of product life cycle was discussed more fully in chapter 6, it is fitting to restate it as a decision factor and expand the concept to include all the Ps. There is a life cycle for products, for pricing, for distribution channels, and for promotional strategies. All come into being in response to customer needs, all have a peak period of effectiveness, and all undergo a period of decline in which further usefulness should be assessed.

This is the normal sequence of events and should be viewed as such. Many information services, particularly libraries, have great difficulty in eliminating a product/service, a distribution point such as a branch, ways of promoting that are marginally effective, or the "free" tag on certain services that might be considered for partial or full cost-recovery. In flush years, it is historically easy to introduce a new service; it is equally difficult to discontinue a service. However, when funds are in shorter supply and hard choices must be made, the concept of life cycle becomes an essential consideration and is critical to understanding that a natural ebb and flow be recognized.

Positioning

Positioning the product within the market is another way to respond to changing conditions. The value of carving out a market share from the total possible market must be stressed in any consideration of distribution methods. Each day we are flooded with messages, information, advertising, and appeals. To make a lasting impression on a customer's mind, an information agency needs to have a clear understanding of what specific product/service is being offered, what benefits would be received, and a way of having customers remember when they are in need of that product/service. That clear understanding can be attained through use of an effective marketing/planning process. However, ensuring that customers remember is more than simple promotion: It is positioning.

For each product of the information agency, a way must be found to position that product in the minds of potential customers. If it is not possible to be number one in an area with a product, in terms of quality or speed or cost, perhaps that product is more effectively handled by another organization. The challenge may be to redesign the product in a unique manner, or identify a product that can claim the number one slot. Finding a unique niche in the market is not easy, but it is definitely worth the effort. For public institutions, cooperation and nonduplication generally create favorable impressions on the part of funding authorities. For private agencies, it is simply good business to seek out a unique market share.

Again, data derived from the marketing audit provide the key to positioning: 1) identify the mission of the organization; 2) identify the market segments; and 3) delineate the products/services that will be addressed to each segment. Once these three steps are accomplished, it is much easier to find the position within the market segment that will reach number one status in terms of that market's needs. Finding the market niche will depend on two factors: what is unique about the product/service and why it is better/faster/cheaper than the competition. It is not uncommon for the creative use of distribution channels to be the deciding element in establishing that market niche.

DISTRIBUTION—PLACING THE PRODUCT

J. Newcomb, in an analysis of electronic information distribution in the publishing industry, sees the challenge as "an attempt to solve a new and complex puzzle with numerous interrelated parts: evaluating the changing information demands within traditional markets and emerging new markets; determining the appropriate distribution vehicle; deciding whether to build the necessary distribution capability or enter into a joint venture; making complex pricing judgments; and changing . . . focuses."[10]

It seems apparent that such a prescription cannot be followed without creative and flexible approaches to information service. It is also evident, according to Arthur Sterngold, that an organization must consciously choose how it positions itself in its marketplace, with decisions made concerning which target groups and which information needs will be satisfied—and through what channels of distribution.[11]

Placing the product in the marketplace in the most favorable position is a complex task, but one in which creativity can play a real role. When correlated to customer information needs, channels of distribution may be designed to enhance the marketability of each information product, thereby increasing the opportunity for achieving the top market position. Of the 4 Ps of the marketing methods, place/distribution may well be the most flexible and responsive to innovation. The possibilities of creative distribution offer a real challenge to the information professional and, perhaps, the "best shot" at meeting customer needs and effectively dealing with tomorrow's world.

Scenario for Further Thought: Place/Distribution

The Beta Public Library is situated in a large metropolitan area that contains human service agencies, as well as a private information service and a major university. The library is fairly typical of a public library with audiovisual materials, art prints and sculpture, a best-seller rental collection, and in-person and telephone service. There is also an active children's program.

The library presently has a central facility with eight branches, plus its telephone reference service.

The local cable company is about to switch over to interactive capability and will also offer Internet connection.

The library staff meets informally on annual goals; no long-range planning is done. A community analysis has been discussed, but never undertaken.

- In an effort to be more effective in the community, the library has just hired a marketing director who is new to the area. What steps should this new staff member take to become acquainted with the library's position and to begin analyzing the distribution possibilities?
- What should be done in the first year, the second year, in five years?
- What possible distribution factors should be considered? Why?

NOTES

1. Darlene E. Weingand, *Customer Service Excellence: A Concise Guide for Librarians* (Chicago: American Library Association, 1997), 33.

2. William A. Band, *Creating Value for Customers: Designing and Implementing a Total Corporate Strategy* (New York: Wiley, 1991), 145–48.

3. Peter Davis, "Libraries at the Turning Point: Issues in Proactive Planning," *Journal of Library Administration* 1, no. 2 (Summer 1980): 11–24.

4. Ibid., 17.

5. Ibid., 20.

6. Darlene E. Weingand, "Distribution of the Library's Product: The Need for Innovation," *Journal of Library Administration* 4, no. 4 (Winter 1984): 49–57.

7. Ibid., 55.

8. Joel A. Barker, *Discovering the Future: The Business of Paradigms,* 2d ed. (Burnsville, Minn.: Infinity and Charthouse, 1989), video.

9. Weingand, "Distribution of the Library's Product," 56.

10. J. Newcomb, "Electronic Information Distribution," *Special Libraries* 74, no. 2 (April 1983): 155.

11. Arthur Sterngold, "Marketing for Special Libraries and Information Centers: The Positioning Process," *Special Libraries* 73, no. 4 (October 1982): 254–59.

Chapter 9

Promotion—Last, but Not Least

ဆာ

The traditional perception of marketing by library staff has been promotion or public relations, without a complete understanding of the scope and depth of the entire marketing/planning process. Further, this perception has been framed in the context of the former paradigm of libraries as a public "good," containing products that are intrinsically valuable and that "should" be used by the community. Such a paradigm suggests that customers need only be alerted to the existence of these library products. But, in addition, promotion has often featured library programmatic activities, such as story hours and film/video showings, rather than upon the full range of services, and the community has not been fully informed as to what benefits the library can provide to enhance daily life. Consequently, most customers have a very poor sense of what they have a right to expect—and demand—from libraries.

Essential to the discussion is an examination of basic promotional philosophy. Promotion has been portrayed both as sales and as education—two very different viewpoints. If the sales view is used, the process resembles the traditional library approach. The sales view presumes that a product currently exists and that mechanisms need to be created to entice potential customers to desire that product: "Build a better mousetrap. . . ." This notion of created desire may seem somewhat artificial, but it has been standard practice in the profit sector for many years. However, even in the business world, the perspective has shifted from creating artificial demand to identifying market needs and wants. Companies do extensive market research in order to determine what these customer needs might be and what products are likely to appeal to potential buyers.

The other philosophical view is that promotion, like lobbying, is an educational activity. Rather than focusing on customer desire (whether real or artificial), the educative approach concentrates on communication of information so that customers may become more knowledgeable and, consequently, better able to make informed decisions. This latter philosophical perspective forms the framework for this chapter, although the market research approach has certainly been covered in the discussion on the marketing audit in chapter 4.

THE FOUNDATION: COMMUNICATION

However, the construct of information organizations presented in this book includes not only libraries but a full spectrum of agencies, both nonprofit and profit. In like manner, the view of *promotion* also needs updating and should be expanded to reflect its true purpose: *communication*. This communication process should reflect an ongoing conversation between the information agency and its present and potential customers, in which community needs are identified and responses developed to address those needs.

Because promotion is intended to facilitate the communication between the information agency and its target markets, a brief look at the communication model will aid in understanding the promotional applications. Philip Kotler describes communication as a framework. In every communication interaction, there is a sender and a receiver, plus other elements of the transaction. The following eight components, illustrated in figure 9.1, are involved in every communication exchange:

- Sender: the party sending the message to another party (also called the source or communicator)

- Encoding: the process of putting thought into symbolic form

- Message: the set of symbols that the sender transmits

- Media (or channels): the paths through which the message moves from sender to receiver

- Decoding: the process by which the receiver assigns meaning to the symbols transmitted by the sender

- Receiver: the party receiving the message sent by another party (also called the audience or destination)

- Response: the set of reactions that the receiver has after being exposed to the message

- Feedback: the part of the receiver's response that the receiver communicates back to the sender[1]

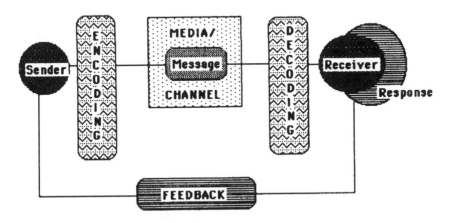

Fig. 9.1. Flow of the communication process.

Figure 9.1 illustrates the flow of the communication process. The jagged lines in the "encoding" and "decoding" components signify static or dissonance, an interruption to the smooth flow of the message. For example, the sender may be fatigued or thinking about next week's vacation when designing the message, or the receiver may be distracted in some way and not fully attend to the message being transmitted. For this reason, incorporating a feedback loop is an essential step.

In order to use the communication model to full advantage, the "sender" information agency must know what target market(s) it wants to reach and what types of responses are desired. The marketing audit should provide data on where specific target markets seek information, such as what newspapers, television channels, or radio stations are normally utilized. The message needs to be transmitted over the most efficient and effective media/channel—media with a history of actually reaching the target market. Sending messages via a channel not frequented by the target market is futile. Skill should also be used in encoding messages that take into account how the target market usually go about decoding messages, and feedback mechanisms must be developed so that the market response to the message can be ascertained.

MAKING IT WORK

Agency resources are admittedly finite, but they are the means through which agency plans and activities move from being abstract ideas into practical application. Without sufficient administrative supports—including funding, staff time, and psychological commitment—the most worthy of ideas will wither.

The appropriate level of support begins with a resolution from the agency's governing body, whether that authority is constituted as a board of directors, board of regents, executive council, school board, or other entity. This resolution, noting that promotion is a long-term, continuous activity, should state a philosophical and financial commitment to the process. It should be written in as specific language as possible, covering such concepts as the need for staff training; cooperation with other agencies, libraries, and groups; a commitment to information-sharing appearances by staff at various times and places in the community; promotional literature; and the designation of a staff member as coordinator.

Beyond this initial resolution lies the daily, weekly, monthly, and annual continuing commitment to effective promotion as an integral part of the agency's marketing/planning effort. This extension of administrative supports from the policy level through the practical daily implementation is basic to successful promotional activities.

Building on this strong foundation of administrative commitment, the agency encounters so many interpretations regarding promotion that its many aspects can be compared to a multifaceted gemstone. This discussion will address several of these aspects, but the list is not inclusive.

1. The first aspect concerns the most common interpretation of promotion: public relations. Many people equate promotion with public relations (PR). This, however, is an incomplete impression and one that significantly undervalues the entire promotional package. As a legitimate component of the promotional effort, public relations is exceedingly important, essentially covering the

ongoing interaction between the information agency and its current and potential target markets. Public relations influences public opinion by conveying information concerning the benefits of using the products offered or proposed.

Two primary avenues of communication under the umbrella term of public relations are *publicity* and *personal contact*. Both avenues attempt to create and maintain a heightened level of awareness on the part of the community.

Publicity involves news coverage at minimum or no cost. Press releases are probably the most frequently used mechanism for generating publicity. Such releases are distributed to appropriate mass media outlets (radio, television, newspapers) and to interested organizations for redistribution (through their newsletters, for example). Other avenues for publicity include the newsletters published by the information agency itself, bookmarks, posters, and displays.

Personal contact is stimulated by means of an informed library staff and possibly (in larger agencies) a designated specialist whose job description includes publicizing agency product lines. Anne Mathews states that "the most effective way to promote any library is through a personable, courteous, efficient, and knowledgeable staff. Everyone who works in a library is considered by the public to be a 'librarian.' Public service personnel must be good salespersons: this includes the pages who shelve books and library technicians, as well as professional and administrative staff. In the selection and training of library personnel, it is important to stress that this is a profession of service to people! Library staff should never hesitate to approach a customer and ask if they may help him or her, and if they don't know the answer, to offer to get someone who may be able to offer assistance. And to keep smiling!"[2]

2. A second aspect of promotion is *advertising*. Advertising is paid publicity, often both sophisticated and expensive. This mechanism, which can be used to increase activity in all four quadrants of figure 7.5, can be focused on current and/or potential products and current and/or potential target markets.

Although advertising needs to be increasingly "slick" in order to attract the consumer's attention and to compete with other advertisements, advertising and publicity may be combined in the form of a "bug." For the publicly supported information agency on a limited budget, a request might be made to a frequent community advertiser to include a small mention or reference to the agency and its product(s) within the normal paid advertisement. For example, a grocery store advertising for a major holiday such as Thanksgiving may be happy to include a small insert stating that the local public library can be helpful in providing menus, decorating hints, and even a "how to" carve the turkey! Such a "bug" can be included not only in newspaper ads, but in television or radio spots as well.

3. *Incentives* are a third aspect of the promotional package. Incentives, generally found in a product's market testing phase, are designed to focus customer attention on a new product and to create goodwill. Sample incentives might be a free online search or faxed article, an extended loan period for videocassettes, a sample SDI (Selective Dissemination of Information) packet of material expertly targeted to the user's interests, a bookmark or button describing a new service, a free demonstration, and so forth.

4. *Atmospherics,* critical to the promotional mix, consists of the ambience and environment of the distribution channels, whether those channels are brick and mortar or electronic transmission. This ambience is designed to produce specific cognitive and affective responses within a target market. Each channel will have a look and a feel that may add or detract from customer satisfaction and staff performance.

In addition to consideration of these aspects and the possible media/channels listed in figure 9.2, there are other approaches that can significantly enhance the promotional mix. These tactics should not be used in isolation, but rather should be merged into the total promotional mix. For example, the importance of third-party endorsement—using community leaders as opinion makers—should be recognized as a powerful promotional tactic and can be observed commercially in the use of celebrities to sell products. It can also be used very nicely in shaping public opinion to view an agency's product in a positive light.

A second approach is the deliberate education of staff members and funding authorities in the rationale and elements of the agency's planning process so that they can be marketing ambassadors. Interpersonal communication, particularly when it comes from a person knowledgeable about the agency and its operations, can be most valuable.

Media/Channels	How My Library/Agency Could Use Them
Press kit	
Photographs	
News releases	
News memo for quick release	
Column item	
Feature story	
News conference	
Special event	
Collateral material: buttons, bookmarks, bumper stickers	
Annual report	
Posters	
Brochures	
Direct mail	
Public service announcements (PSAs)	
Newsletters	
Speeches/public appearances	
Media presentations	

Fig. 9.2. Examples of possible media/channels for reaching target market.

Personalizing the service so that customers readily identify with and relate to the products is a third approach. Removing barriers associated with time and distance, while adding more personal touches, can make customers feel more valued, comfortable, and connected to the agency.

Stressing present and potential benefits, a fourth approach, enables customers to envision the results of using the product(s). This focus on benefits has been emphasized repeatedly in this book, but its importance is such that it warrants emphasis here as well.

A fifth approach is cross-selling: Stimulating customer interest in additional information, possibly in related topics or different formats. For example, if a customer is interested in Icelandic folklore, he or she might be offered (in addition to books on folklore) some videos, pictorial reproductions, descriptive and historical information on Iceland, and referral to persons having experience with the country and/or the language.

Finally, the development of tangible symbols for promotional activities can create an image for both the product and the agency. An agency logo should be created, which would then appear on all presentation materials used by the agency. All staff should carry—and generously distribute—business cards that display the logo and contact information for the agency. Creative and consistent use of a logo, special color, and unique designs can help to make identifying connections in the customer's memory.

These aspects and approaches give substance and form to the discussion of promotion, but promotion as a process is not undertaken in a vacuum. Referring back to figure 1.3, it can be seen that promotion is part of the implementation of action strategies. Unless promotional activities are integrated both conceptually and practically into the planning process, they may actually frustrate the achievement of stated goals and objectives. It is imperative for the planning team to keep each part of the planning process in perspective vis-à-vis the total effort.

DESIGNING THE PUBLIC INFORMATION PLAN

With the framework of the communication model firmly in mind and a sense for the various facets of promotion that should be considered, it becomes possible to adapt the principles of promotion directly to the information agency's public information plan (PIP). Such a plan provides the structure upon which various promotional efforts can be attached. The PIP enables the agency to develop a coordinated and interrelated design for communicating with its customers.

The first step is to explain the agency's rationale for its products: what the agency does and why. This rationale should be based on the findings of the marketing audit and the demonstrated needs that the audit has identified. Further explication of the rationale would focus on benefits—the precise benefits that customer use of the agency's product(s) would reap.

The second step consists of the basic communication questions:

1. *What is to be communicated? (Message)*
   The planning team needs to be aware of how this message correlates to the agency's goals, objectives, and priorities.

2. *Why?*
   The organizational mission should be able to provide the response to this question.

3. *To whom? (Receiver)*
   The message must be directed to discrete target markets.

4. *How? (Media / Channels)*
   The importance of a good relationship with the various media is paramount. These mass media connections may include, but are not limited to, weekly and daily newspapers, magazines, television and radio stations, and the library press. There are numerous channels for reaching the target market(s), many of which are listed in figure 9.2. Tests for selection of appropriate media/channels can be condensed into the following questions:

   • Will it reach the target market(s)?

   • Will the market be receptive to the message?

   • Can the agency create/develop the type of media to carry the message?

   • Can the agency afford the cost?

   • Can the selected media get the message out fast enough?

   • Is there any possibility that the choice of media could produce negative consequences? Could untargeted markets also receive the message and misinterpret its intent?

   These questions are predicated on the assumption that the agency has already conducted its marketing audit and identified its target markets, its own strengths and limitations, and so forth. Selection of appropriate media is an activity introduced toward the final stages of a planning cycle; essentially, it ties together all the information and efforts that have already been accomplished by the planning team.

5. *Who has the responsibility?*
   Although it is the final communication question, the query about responsibility is by no means less important. If an agency can afford to designate a full-time person

to handle either promotion or the entire marketing/ planning effort, this is ideal. More often, however, these tasks will become one part of a staff member's job description. What is critical, though, is that one person be put in charge so that coordination of this multifaceted operation is effectively accomplished.

It is no easy matter to design and carry out a successful public information plan, but it is a crucial component in a successful marketing/planning process. The challenge of developing an effective communication plan, a far-reaching goal for the agency, is definitely worth the expenditure of agency resources.

Finally, all of these efforts must be built upon honesty and trust—qualities that transform promotion into ongoing effective public relations. Whatever strategies are designed and implemented, honesty and trust should be a "given" in the minds of both agency personnel and target markets. Without this basic trust, promotional results may be fleeting. When honesty and trust are operative and benefits to the customer are clearly defined, promotion can be one of the truly joyous parts of the marketing/planning process.

Scenario for Further Thought: Promotion

Within commuting distance from a state capital of 150,000 population, two communities of 15,000 residents established public libraries. Both library directors are interested in promoting library services to their communities, but are approaching the process in different ways. Discuss the probable success and failure of the strategies selected by these two library directors:

Library A

No formal marketing/planning process

Director regards the library as a storehouse of knowledge

Ninety-nine percent of the collection is books

Director proposes to use the following promotional strategies:

- Newspaper column to be written by director
- Posters
- Displays
- Class visits
- No budget to be allocated to promotion because times are tough

Library B

Just completing the first planning process ever attempted

Director regards the library as a node in a vast information network

Collection contains a mix of media formats

Director proposes to use the following promotional strategies:

- Commitment of agency resources to promotional activities
- Designation of staff member as coordinator
- Press releases
- "Bug" in local grocery ads
- Pilot project of free online searches
- Targeted newsletters directed to specific target markets
- Contacts to be made to agency personnel in the community
- Schedule of speaking engagements

NOTES

1.   Philip Kotler, *Marketing for Nonprofit Organizations,* 2d ed. (Englewood Cliffs, N.J.: Prentice-Hall, 1982), 355.

2.   Anne J. Mathews, "The Use of Marketing Principles in Library Planning," in *Marketing for Libraries and Information Agencies,* ed. Darlene E. Weingand (Norwood, N.J.: Ablex, 1984), 12.

Chapter 10

Evaluation—Two Approaches

"Evaluation" distresses people. The word conjures up images of numbers, mathematics, measurement, and other things that humanities-based professionals view with fear and loathing. Although more and more social science and science graduates are entering information work, there still lingers an underlying distaste for the numerical side of evaluation activities. In this light, a more positive view can be to ask instead, "Is it working?" or "How good is it?" Answers to these questions can be learned through quantitative measures, but also through more qualitative means such as stories. With the marketing/planning effort, evaluation asks these questions in relation to the established criteria of goals and objectives.

WHY EVALUATE?

There are many reasons to evaluate. In *The TELL IT! Manual,* Debra Wilcox Johnson provides a detailed and useful list:

- Someone required it
- Monitors progress to allow for program adjustment
- Provides baseline information for comparison over time
- Aids with decision making to:
  Adjust a program
  Continue a program
  Discontinue a program
  Allocate funds among programs

- It's part of planning
- Makes more systematic our natural tendency to assess
- Allows a library to affect how it is evaluated
- Aids communication with different stakeholders (i.e., staff, funders, users)
- Assures participants have a voice in a program
- Provides insight and information that can lead to answers
- Gives a fresh perspective
- Provides supporting information for grant proposals
- Gives a view of what's working and what's not
- Tests assumptions about approaches or client groups
- Documents outcomes or impacts
- Makes sense of messes[1]

In other words, <u>evaluation is a tool for improving services, not simply a scorecard.</u>

The purpose of evaluation is not just to know whether to feel good about some aspect of the library/information agency's operations. Its purpose is to allow managers to make better decisions, to identify aspects of service that might be improved, and to target functions that need to be speeded up or made less expensive.[2]

Robbins-Carter and Zweizig have identified seven common-sense elements in the evaluation process:

1. Determine the target area.
2. Set the target.
3. How will you know?
4. Take a look.
5. How close are you?
6. So what?
7. Rethink.[3]

In each of these seven elements, the planning team steps back to view the marketing/planning effort (or any targeted portion) from a slightly different perspective.

1. *Determine the target area.*

2. *Set the target.*

The question is asked: "What do we want to accomplish and how well?" These steps are appropriately integrated into the objective-setting and action phases of the marketing/planning process. Decisions are made as to what the library/information agency will attempt to accomplish. By writing the objective and action statements in measurable or observable terms, the evaluation mechanism is firmly in place.

3. *How will you know?*

For the purposes of final evaluation, the measurable approach to objective and action statement setting makes the result obvious. However, the monitoring requirements of process evaluation may make the defining of specific data collection procedures necessary. (Such procedures may be either quantitative or qualitative in approach.)

4. *Take a look.*

5. *How close are you?*

An obvious extension to number three, these elements ask that the data collected for monitoring purposes be examined to make a comparison between the target set in the objective and the actual progress that has been accomplished. Progress may be as projected, or greater or less than projected. Minutes should be kept of the planning team's deliberations and any decisions that are taken so that the process is tracked and used to inform the next planning cycle.

6. *So what?*

7. *Rethink.*

These seven elements form a practical framework upon which to build an evaluation effort. The hoped-for result is improvement of library/information agency service effectiveness.

THE ANATOMY OF EVALUATION

Therefore, if service improvement is the ultimate purpose of evaluation, there must logically be a link between evaluation and effectiveness. Childers and Van House have examined the management literature and have concluded that there are four main approaches to looking at organizational effectiveness. These different viewpoints focus on different aspects about the organization and are presented as questions, followed by this author's comments:

- *To what extent does the organization achieve its goals?*

This question looks at the library/information agency's goals, objectives, and actions. If the objectives and actions have been written in measurable terms, the assessment of effectiveness is relatively straightforward.

- *To what extent is the organization a healthy operating unit?*

The marketing audit forms the baseline for this measure of effectiveness. Analysis of the internal environment provides the data necessary to evaluate organizational health.

- *To what extent can the organization capture from the external environment the resources needed to survive or thrive?*

The marketing audit, by comparative examination of external environment capabilities and internal ability to attract resources, can help to reach conclusions about this essential question of resource allocation.

- *To what extent are the various stakeholders' priorities met?*[4]

Audit of the external environment and subsequent identification of customer needs and wants can provide important clues for consideration of this question.

These questions are central to the consideration of evaluating agency effectiveness. However, evaluation needs to be approached on two levels: monitoring effectiveness and rendering final judgment.

Types of Evaluation

There are two approaches to evaluation: process (formative) and summary (summative). These two approaches work quite nicely into the whole marketing/planning process. Process evaluation monitors progress toward fulfilling goals and objectives (see chapter 5), whereas summary evaluation delivers the verdict at the end of a specified time period or project, judging whether or not the goals and objectives were, in fact, achieved and in a timely way.

Process (Formative) Evaluation

In the monitoring mode, process evaluation measures the progress that is being made toward fulfilling the library/information agency's objectives. An analogy might be drawn between process evaluation and daily quizzes in school. The purpose of the daily quiz is to keep an eye on development, on the movement toward a goal. Affecting interim decisions, this mode of evaluation may have one of the following impacts: 1) it may call for minor adjustments or fine-tuning of the marketing plan and planning document; 2) it may indicate a substantial change of direction; or 3) it may indicate a completely new approach. This monitoring process results in fewer mistakes en route, with fewer failures at the end.

In *The TELL IT! Manual,* Debra Wilcox Johnson highlights two points: "1) that evaluation information is collected throughout the life of a project or throughout a planning cycle and 2) that evaluation information can be used to help keep a project or service 'on track' toward reaching the desired outcomes."[5] This allows for mid-course corrections and adjustments, as appropriate.

As the planning team monitors progression toward achieving an objective, the following questions should be asked:

1. Are current measurement techniques adequately monitoring the rate of progress toward the objective? Should additional data be collected? How?

2. Is the movement toward achieving the objective on target? [Is it] behind or ahead of schedule? Are the expectations of progress still realistic?

3. Should additional or different strategies be developed?

4. Should pilot projects be expanded to the entire organization? Should experimental strategies be continued, expanded, or discontinued?

5. Are the costs running close to original estimates? Are they adversely affecting any other objectives?

6. Is the overachievement in any area adversely affecting other objectives or encumbering a disproportionate amount of resources?

7. Is the objective becoming unrealistic or proving undesirable in the overall picture? Should it be modified or eliminated?

8. Should new objectives be developed to better achieve particular goals?

9. Is the objective still relevant to the information agency's defined role in terms of itself and its community? Have any environmental factors changed?

10. Is the development of new objectives or goals indicated to meet changing needs?

11. Finally, should the priority ranking among goals and objectives be revised?[6]

Careful consideration of these questions as the marketing/planning process proceeds should keep it on track.

Between Major Planning Surges. Although process evaluation is an ongoing activity and is directly tied to planning objectives and actions, it can be a reasonable and cost-effective effort if it is overseen by a designated committee consisting of agency staff and a subset of the original planning team. The extensive time commitment required of the original planning team is key to beginning an effective marketing/planning process. However, the data secured from the first marketing audit can be considered valid for several years—or until major internal or external change occurs. Once the first planning cycle has been completed with the final evaluation submitted, the original large planning team may be reconstituted into a smaller working committee to plan and monitor successive cycles until environmental conditions (internal and/or external) indicate that another full marketing audit is required. A reasonable rule of thumb is to allow a maximum of three to five years before another full audit is conducted, unless changing conditions mandate otherwise.

The responsibilities and tasks of this interim monitoring committee include:

1. Meeting regularly and at least quarterly.

2. Monitoring progress and recommending alterations when necessary.

3. Monitoring pilot projects.

4. Making recommendations concerning future objectives and strategies.

5. Identifying needed data to be collected and designating personnel to be responsible.

6. Securing periodic input from target markets.

7. Disseminating collected data.

8. Monitoring resource allocations.

9. Evaluating progress and modifying the plan as necessary.[7]

These are important ingredients in the total marketing/ planning process. It would be poor accountability to invest resources in such a process and then simply launch it without building in the essential process evaluation piece. The committee members charged with the monitoring role are invested with an important trust.

To fulfill the above responsibilities, the committee should consider the following questions:

- Has the plan's success or failure reaffirmed or challenged the agency's chosen role in the community?

- Has agency performance improved?

- Have changes occurred in either the internal or external environments?

- Have any unforeseen problems or opportunities arisen?[8]

In considering these lists of tasks, responsibilities, and questions, it is clear that the interim planning committee must devote close attention to the workings of the marketing/planning activities and either recommend or make adjustments as appropriate. Through this ongoing, systematic process of monitoring evaluation, the marketing/planning efforts will proceed smoothly, with administrative decision making based on forethought and hard data.

Final (Summative) Evaluation

This mode of evaluation is the type that most people focus on when thinking about evaluation. It is related to the popular concept of the "bottom line." Questions to be asked include:

1. Is it a success or a failure?

2. Are the results positive or negative?

3. Will we want to do it again?

4. Was it worthwhile?

5. Should we do it again? Can we? When?

6. What can/should be changed to improve the next attempt?

These questions will lead the planning team into discussions, and ultimately into decisions, regarding the agency's goals and objectives. In this discussion, it should be determined which objectives and/or actions need repeating, reworking, or, ideally, have been fulfilled. The time and responsibility designations written into each objective and action strategy will enable the final evaluation to be done easily and painlessly. Discussion should include not only the obvious result of whether or not an objective or action target was achieved, but also whether the companion process evaluation indicated that adjustments need to be made.

Evaluation can be compared, expanding upon the analogy of the roadmap introduced in chapter 5, to an automobile journey from New York to San Francisco. In process evaluation, the map is checked frequently to see if the right roads are being selected and followed. (One would not want to wind up in New Orleans if the goal were to reach San Francisco!) In summary evaluation, an assessment is made that determines whether, at journey's end, the car had reached San Francisco and within the time span originally allotted.

ROLES AND RESPONSIBILITIES

Both approaches to evaluation do two things: gather information and compare what is learned to a set of criteria. The criteria for either monitoring or final judgment should be multifaceted and relate directly to the library/information agency's goals and objectives—as well as to the four questions listed above. What has been learned from the marketing audit forms the information base.

The library/information agency director and staff are responsible for providing this information base, as they are responsible for the ongoing measurement and evaluation of the services they provide. Timely and relevant evaluative information must be gathered by those who are involved in the day-to-day implementation of activities: agency staff members. In order to successfully fulfill this responsibility, they need a basic understanding of measurement and evaluation and must also understand how to develop measures, how to collect data, and how to analyze those data.

Most planning team members are not interested in learning measurement techniques in any depth. However, they can effectively participate in the activities required to select the most meaningful measures of progress toward reaching a goal.[9] The planning team assists the staff in interpreting the gathered information, using it to improve decision making about future directions.

Evidence can be gathered by the agency staff in several ways:

- *Quantitative evidence.* From both secondary sources (data that has already been collected by another agency) and primary sources (surveys, interviews, questionnaires, etc.). Because each objective and action statement has both completion time and responsibility designations, charts can be made showing employees' responsibilities and progress, including the planned and actual starting and completion dates.

- *Qualitative evidence.* Generated from such sources as focus groups, observation, documentation of stories reflecting the library/information agency's effect on customers and their lives. Personal observation by an activity's implementor may clarify why an activity succeeds or fails. Insights come from considering such questions as:

  1. What contributed to the success or failure of the activity?

  2. Was anything overlooked in planning the steps to conduct this activity?

  3. Were there any unanticipated results?

  4. What could have been done differently?[10]

Once the planning team has gathered the evaluation data and compared progress with original targets, decisions must be made concerning possible adjustments in the plan and/or major changes in direction. It is very useful to chart actual accomplishments against the level of accomplishment proposed in the objectives and action plans. The experience of analyzing both targets and evaluation data results in a decision-making process that is proactive rather than reactive—in other words, the result is better management.

IN A NUTSHELL

Evaluation may be a formal investigation or an intuitive assessment—or both. It becomes easier with experience and practice. Although it is an ongoing process, it does reach plateaus of either time (the end of a particular strategy or project, the conclusion of a fiscal year) or activity (as an objective is accomplished). These plateaus mark the point at which process evaluation changes into summary evaluation and monitoring becomes judgment. In effect, evaluation nurtures the marketing/planning process; conversely, the process also prompts evaluation.

A summary prescription for effective evaluation can be expressed in these four lines:

- Measure performance and results throughout the process.

- Adjust the process as evaluation indicates.

- Document all changes and their rationale.

- Chart directions for the future.

And finally, a proverb to remember: "Evaluation is the glue that holds the marketing/planning effort together."

In the next and final chapter, the concepts of marketing/planning presented thus far are funneled into a future-oriented discussion of how present success can influence tomorrow's effectiveness.

Scenario for Further Thought: Evaluation

The Omega Information Service is approaching the midpoint of the first year of its initial marketing/planning effort. Omega serves small businesses in a city of 150,000 people that is within three hours of a major metropolitan area.

- The targets projected in the Omega objectives are behind schedule by nearly 30 percent.

- In addition, rumor has it that the local automotive plant, which employs 35 percent of the city's workforce, may be slated to close.

- The good news is that the city council, actively seeking growth in the business community, is courting several companies for possible relocation to the area.

- How should the members of the planning team for Omega structure their evaluation procedures at this time in order to obtain the most reliable information for decision making?

- Do the projected environmental changes indicate the need for another marketing audit?

- Should the planning team consider evaluation of Omega services alone or should they make recommendations based on the larger community profile?

NOTES

1. Debra Wilcox Johnson, "Training Outlines and Guidelines," in Douglas Zweizig and others, *The TELL IT! Manual: The Complete Program for Evaluating Library Performance* (Chicago: American Library Association, 1996), 70.

2. Jane Robbins-Carter and Douglas L. Zweizig, "Are We There Yet?" *American Libraries* 16, no. 9 (October 1985): 624.

3. Ibid., 625–26.

4. Thomas A. Childers and Nancy A. Van House, *What's Good? Describing Your Public Library's Effectiveness* (Chicago: American Library Association, 1993), 7.

5. Wilcox Johnson, "Training Outlines and Guidelines," 76.

6. Vernon E. Palmour, Marcia C. Bellassai, and Nancy V. DeWath, *A Planning Process for Public Libraries* (Chicago: American Library Association, 1980), 81.

7. Ibid., 83.

8. Mike Jaugstetter and Janice Williams, *Strategy Development and Evaluation, Long Range Planning for Public Libraries,* Occasional Paper Series 1, no. 6 (Columbus, Ohio: State Library of Ohio, n.d.), 4.

9. Ethel Himmel and William James Wilson, *Planning for Results: A Public Library Transformation Process* (Chicago: American Library Association, 1998), 64.

10. Jaugstetter and Williams, *Strategy Development,* 3–4.

℅

Chapter 11

Present Success—And Designing a Preferred Future

℘ ————————————————————

This volume has established a foundation for developing a marketing/planning system and presented a discussion of each step of the process. This final chapter provides additional points to consider to help ensure the success of the marketing/planning effort.

ANOTHER LOOK AT VISION

The future is not predetermined. We have continuous opportunities to influence its development and, therefore, its evolution. Designing a preferred future involves three approaches: envisioning the parameters of the desired outcome, working toward that outcome, and working against those futures that are less appealing. Envisioning is both the first and the most important step, as it forms the foundation for the other two approaches.

Ellen Altman proposes that the "vision thing" requires a willingness to consider letting go of the familiar and to change. She challenges librarians to ask themselves whether they "should continue to regard libraries primarily as places where commercially produced information/entertainment packages are stores awaiting selection, or as systems which can deliver entertainment, information, or learning specifically to meet customer requirements."[1] She suggests five skills that might serve information professionals into a new millennium:

- an understanding of customer preferences for information that, in turn, drives the selection of inventory;

- an understanding of information-seeking behavior that facilitates users' successful retrieval;

- the ability to identify materials appropriate to customers' requirements and their ability to understand them;

- the ability to advise customers who have questions about related materials, reliability, accuracy, and author authority;

- the ability to identify, understand, and access information environments beyond commercially produced materials from mainstream vendors.[2]

These emphases on both customers and information transfer are central to creating a vision for the future. Customer focus requires that we consider customers in the context of lifestyles and the changes that may be just ahead.

LIBRARIES, CUSTOMERS, AND LIFESTYLE CHANGES

Customer service issues most frequently focus on the exchange between the library/information agency and its customers. The proactive library embraces change and the opportunities that are inevitably presented. In such a dynamic environment, the library becomes a learning organization, purposefully reinventing itself to meet present and anticipated customer needs. Customer convenience and information-seeking behavior are prime directives for developing products and services.

However, libraries and information agencies are also inevitably linked to customer lifestyles, as customers are three-dimensional human beings. Yet, too often, staff members may generalize across a target market, or perhaps even mentally assign individual customers to categorized compartments. Because each customer is a unique individual, this can be misleading at best and potentially disastrous when customer needs and wants are being identified.

Therefore, a look at potential changes in lifestyles can be useful. The following list reflects a sampling of potential changes that was compiled by two advertising professionals in 1997. The reader should note that this is a selected list, which includes those projections that seem more relevant to information service than others appearing on the comprehensive list. However, all changes that do occur will ultimately result in some level of impact upon libraries and information agencies.[3]

Home

- Company towns will reemerge . . .
- Community personal assistants will be hired by community groups and neighbors who will pool their resources . . .
- Living in the global village . . .
- "Special purpose" rooms will be in demand . . .
- Intelligent wallpapers turn every flat surface into an art gallery . . . television/computer screen . . .
- Virtual aquariums or scenic vistas . . .
- Soundproofed rooms will be in demand . . .

Family and Education

- Coparenting initiatives . . .
- Cyber-Spock: The Internet . . . parenting and childcare advice and resources . . .
- "Nannycams" hidden inside teddy bears . . .
- Ankle or wrist monitors for kids . . .
- Enforced parental responsibility . . . for children's misbehavior . . .
- In-home videoconferencing . . . to stay in touch . . .
- Networked schooling with increased cooperation—and competition . . .
- Bilingual daycare centers and preschools . . .
- Entrepreneur camps for teenagers . . .
- Spirituality-based camps and clubs . . .
- Virtual libraries . . .

Leisure and Socializing

- Simple pleasures from times past, such as sewing and quilting bees . . .

- Comfort foods rather than sophisticated gourmet meals . . .

- "Dinner clubs" . . .

- Meals-on-wheels for the masses: [in] minivans and other family vehicles . . .

- Holographic storage . . . expanded home video library . . .

- Computer-generated friendship circles . . . identify people around the world . . . share common interests . . .

- Matchmakers for friendships . . .

Health and Wellness

- Food phobia—fear of processed foods and pesticides . . . greater consumption of organic foods . . .

- Nutrition-on-wheels . . . delivery of an assortment of nutritious frozen meals to busy households once a week . . .

- Kid-friendly foods . . .

- Alternative health providers . . .

- Telemedicine linking doctors and patients by videophone . . .

- Diseases spreading more rapidly around the globe . . .

- "Sick building" syndrome generating more complaints . . . telecommuting as an option . . .

Economy and Technology

- Cyber secretaries . . . intelligent agents . . . collecting news and information . . .

- House calls by computer repairers . . .

- Electronic migrant workers: telecommuters . . .

- Portable hard drives . . .

- "Packaged" holidays . . . hiring entrepreneurs to decorate . . . packaged holiday meals . . .

- Personal shoppers . . .

- Nonstop strip malls . . . twenty-four-hour . . .
- Electric cars . . .
- Airports as destinations . . .
- "Underdog" companies flourish, embracing newly introduced technologies . . .
- Values increasingly influence business decisions . . .
- Sabbaticals become standard . . .

These projections cover a wide range of slices of life. Yet, the library/information agency also interacts with multiple life facets, and staff must stay on the "awareness edge" of what is evolving so that customer needs can be addressed. It is clear that many changes are anticipated by the professional trend-watchers; it is equally clear that "tuning in" to developments is an important component of good marketing/planning practice. There is a saying that appears on bumper stickers and T-shirts: "Unless you're the lead dog, the scenery never changes." In terms of libraries, it is the innovative and entrepreneurial library staff that can see the entire landscape of both today and what lies ahead—because they are out in front of the pack!

INFORMATION TRANSFER

The second emphasis centers on how information is accessed and utilized by customers. In their new book, *Blur: The Speed of Change in the Connected Economy,* Stann Davis and Christopher Meyer discuss the "trinity of the blur": connectivity, speed, and intangibles. They offer a list of fifty ways to "Blur Your Business." Although the intended audience for these suggestions are for-profit businesses, some of the ideas can be directly applied to libraries and information agencies:[4]

- *Make speed your mind-set.*

Connecting customers with the information they are seeking involves not only accuracy, but also speed. Customers are interested in immediate service, with speed being part of their definition of excellence.

- *Connect everything with everything.*

In today's global economy, information is an essential resource. Since every library is its community's window to this international marketplace, the establishment of multiple electronic and human connections is essential to success.

- *Grow your intangibles faster than your tangibles.*

Tangible information packages are used for housing information; however, it is the corollary group of intangibles—speed, accuracy, use of equipment, referral, staff friendliness, etc.—that not only enhance the tangible product, but also make it "special" in the eyes of the customer.

- *Build product into every service . . . Put service into every product.*

It is not always recognized that service is automatically part of the product. How the product can be accessed, consideration of customer convenience, communication between staff and customer—all these attributes and more are part of the augmentation aspect of product development. (See chapter 6.) However, poor service is also possible and staff need to strive to achieve the highest level of customer service in order to provide the best-quality product.

- *Manage all business in real time.*

Customers are interested in having their needs met today. While delay is sometimes inevitable, the goal must be to connect the customer and the product in as compressed a time frame as possible.

- *Be able to do anything you do at anytime . . . Be able to do anything, anyplace.*

This is a keystone of access and is rooted firmly in the concept of customer convenience. Such an approach transcends the limitations of time and place, focusing on customer preferences.

- *Put your offer online.*

In today's electronic world, where the number of Web sites proliferate daily, the library/information agency that is not actively involved in this environment has fallen significantly behind the competition. Cutting-edge service requires electronic participation.

- *Make your offer interactive.*

However, a simple Web presence is no longer sufficient. Customers seek the ability to interact with the library's catalog, place holds on materials, initiate electronic reference requests, and so forth. Interactivity is essential to full electronic participation.

- *Customize every offer.*

Ten pages of citations are excessive when three pertinent ones are a better response. Customer convenience requires that the potential responses to a request be filtered in order to provide succinct and targeted information. Customers have constraints on personal time and appreciate professional analysis of information needs.

- *Make sure your offer gets smarter with use.*

As staff members become more experienced with searching databases and delineating the information that customers are seeking, the response to requests should become more targeted and analytical.

- *Make sure your offer anticipates your customers' desires.*

Library hours, parking spaces, online access—these are some of the arenas in which customer desires need to be anticipated. In addition, provision of SDI (Selective Dissemination of Information), which identifies the problems and projects that customers are working on and delivers information/materials in advance of being asked, is an important and valued service.

- *Help your customers get smarter every time they use your offer.*

If customers recognize that they have received a high quality of service and perceive that their information needs have been met, they become not only "smarter" but also inclined to take the next information request to the library.

- *Extract information from every buy/sell exchange.*

As each information request is analyzed by staff, more can be learned about the customer and his/her present and future needs. The Socratic method of eliciting responses can be a very useful tool and what is learned can be used to improve library collections/services/programs and, therefore, better serve the customer at the next encounter.

- *Remember: Every sale is an economic, informational, and emotional exchange.*

But not only information is the content of the customer-staff exchange. There are also implications for the expense of resources (economic, time, human) and the human emotions that accompany the transaction. As long as people are involved, this multidimensional model is in play.

- *Put emotions into every offer and every exchange.*

This is an asset rather than a liability. Human emotions give color to what might have been an otherwise monochromatic transaction. However, we should recognize that this color might be either bright or dark, related to whether the emotional exchange is positive or negative. Positive emotional overtones can bring warmth and energy to the exchange, which definitely adds value.

- *Virtual location, virtual location, virtual location.*

As discussed above, an electronic—or virtual—presence is essential for the library that wishes to stay current with technological and social developments. While change has been described as "perpetual white water" and makes many staff members uneasy, it can also be an exciting challenge. Moving into an electronic environment is a giant step for many libraries, but it is one that is essential.

- *Learn to partner . . .*

Resources are limited. This reality is beyond dispute. The proactive and enterprising organization will seek ways to cooperate and collaborate—and thereby share resources—with other entities. Libraries have a history of partnership that needs to be expanded into the future.

- *Churn to evolve . . . Value what's moving, not what's standing still.*

Inertia is counterproductive and inhibits growth. If the library/information agency wishes to "stay ahead of the pack" (as mentioned earlier), it cannot remain still and rooted in the present. A dynamic, churning environment keeps the organizational juices flowing and ideas generating—a necessary prescription for forward movement.

- *Tear down your firewalls.*

Over time, libraries, as other organizations, have often built firewalls of tradition, assumptions, and other qualities stemming from past practice. A dynamic environment requires fluidity and the ability to combine and recombine in various ways depending upon circumstances.

- *Prize intellectual assets most, financial assets second, physical assets least.*

Intellectual assets are found in staff, who can also be categorized as financial assets because the staff line is the largest budget line in any library/information agency. The physical building and collection are important, but not primary. A proactive perspective will keep these priorities in order.

- *Manage, measure, and grow your intangible capital.*

What is intangible capital? It can be described, in part, as excellence in the augmented product; a friendly, competent, and helpful staff; active listening; positive nonverbal communication; and a focus on customer service.

- *Pay attention. Attention is the next scarce resource.*

The rate of change continues to escalate. Everyone is pushed and pulled by things to do, places to be, deadlines to meet . . . it's a volatile, stress-filled existence. Paying attention may be viewed as a luxury that time does not permit, but it is an essential strategy for success.

While this is a selected list, highlighting those elements viewed as most transferable by this author, the concepts are definitely worth taking very seriously. The world is increasingly complex, and the library/information agency has much to offer its customers in terms of coping skills, necessary information, and a customer-friendly environment.

THE UNKNOWN

Rapid change makes people nervous. Too often, fear becomes an inhibitor that short-circuits professional and personal growth. However, it is not the unknown that is the genesis of uncertainty; it is the interpretation of the unknown. Like crisis, which is simply the convergence of a series of events that makes a decision necessary, the unknown is value-neutral. It is like a blank screen upon which we project our own emotional and imaginative concerns.

Psychologist Wallace Wilkins suggests that we create our own fears by projecting our own frightful images, anticipations, beliefs, and thoughts upon that blank screen. When the projected image is negative or threatening, we are frightened. When it is tragic anticipation, we feel sadness and dread. Conversely, if we project an upbeat, optimistic scene, we create confidence and feel uplifted.[5]

It is a paradox. When we generate our own fears and tragic scenarios, we are unconsciously convinced that we know what is going to happen—which makes the unknown known. A truly unknown future can be interpreted as either negative or positive—with the consequent dreaded or optimistic outcomes. Whether it is personal or organizational planning that is being considered, there are wonderful opportunities to be created if we focus on positive presumptions.

In addition, most library planning has been done based on a single set of assumptions about the future. Because every future is filled with multiple possibilities or alternatives, selecting just one to plan for the future has proved to be both inaccurate and limiting. Incorporating scenario building into the planning process would enable library staff to explore more fully a spectrum of "what ifs."[6]

If we are to move confidently into an uncertain future, considering a pair of questions can be helpful:

"What challenges could the world present me?"

"How might others respond to my actions?"

Creating scenarios around these two questions help us to take the long view, help us recognize and adapt to changing aspects of our present environment, and articulate the different paths that tomorrow might bring. Choices are made today with some understanding of how they might turn out.[7]

TOMORROW AND TOMORROW . . .

The twenty-first century organization is characterized by responsibility, autonomy, risk, and uncertainty[8]—and the library/information agency is an organization. The rigid structures of the Industrial Age organization are giving way to an operating climate that is messy, challenging, and full of advantages and disappointments. Even in an age of heightened technology, this climate is controlled by human beings. Such an organization may not be as predictable and neat as the former model, but it will be a lot more interesting!

Finally, we need to assess the relative "health" of our information organization as we move into the next century. Consultant Richard Beckhard has developed a profile of a healthy organization, with the following attributes:[9]

- Defines itself as a system with known stakeholders

- Has a strong sensing mechanism for receiving [self-analysis] information

- Has a strong sense of purpose and vision

- Operates in "form follows function"—work to be done determines structures and mechanisms

- Employs team management

- Respects customer service as a principle
- Has an information-driven management
- Encourages decisions to be made at the level closest to the customer
- Keeps communication relatively open
- Designs reward systems to be congruent with the work and to support individual development
- Operates in a learning mode
- Recognizes innovation and creativity
- Has a high tolerance for different thinking styles and ambiguity
- Has policies reflecting respect for tensions between work and family demands
- Keeps an explicit social agenda
- Gives sufficient attention to efficient work, quality, and identifying/managing change

Becoming a "healthy organization" is a process of experimentation, risk taking, and scenario building. The library/information agency must examine its relationship to the community it serves and develop a philosophy of service that is developed over time with attention to these questions:

What does the library mean to the staff and to its customers?

What do the library staff members and the library's customers expect from the library?

Where does the library "fit" in the overall community environment?

Where does the staff want it to fit? Does the community share this view?[10]

The library/information agency that will not just "survive" but will "thrive" as we enter the next millennium will be that organization that looks enthusiastically forward—building upon the strong traditions of the past, but not being limited by them. The proactive library will have a staff that views the unknown in a positive light, full of opportunities and promise. Marketing and planning tools will be used regularly to connect with stakeholders and to inform decision making.

It is an exciting time to be an information professional. The possibilities seem endless and the future will be what we make of it. This second edition of *Marketing/Planning Library and Information Services* has reaffirmed the importance of marketing and planning in the managerial process, while recognizing that the future and the present are connected. Vision . . . information . . . customer service: These are keys to unlocking a preferred future, and there are choices to be made.

NOTES

1. Ellen Altman, "The Vision Thing," *Public Libraries* 37, no. 3 (May/June 1998): 158.

2. Ibid., 162.

3. Marian Salzman and Ira Matathia, "Lifestyles of the Next Millennium: 65 Forecasts," *The Futurist* 32, no. 5 (June/July 1998), special insert.

4. Stann Davis and Christopher Meyer. *Blur: The Speed of Change in the Connected Economy* (Reading, Mass.: Addison-Wesley, 1998), 214–37.

5. Wallace Wilkins, "Overcoming Fear of the Unknown," *The Futurist* 32, no. 7 (October 1998): 60.

6. Darlene E. Weingand, *Future-Driven Library Marketing* (Chicago: American Library Association, 1998), 85.

7. Peter Schwartz, *The Art of the Long View: Planning for the Future in an Uncertain World* (New York: Currency Doubleday, 1996), 3–4.

8. Michael Hammer, "The Soul of the New Organization," in *The Organization of the Future,* eds. Frances Hesselbein, Marshall Goldsmith, and Richard Beckhard (San Francisco: Jossey-Bass, 1997), 31.

9. Richard Beckhard, "The Healthy Organization: A Profile," in *The Organization of the Future,* 326–28.

10. Weingand, *Future-Driven Library Marketing,* 29.

BIBLIOGRAPHY

Albritton, Rosie L., and Thomas W. Shaughnessy. *Developing Leadership Skills: A Source Book for Librarians*. Englewood, Colo.: Libraries Unlimited, 1990.

Altman, Ellen. "The Vision Thing." *Public Libraries* 37, no. 3 (May/June 1998): 158.

American Heritage Dictionary. 2d college ed. Boston: Houghton Mifflin, 1982.

Ayres, R. *Technological Forecasting and Long Range Planning*. New York: McGraw-Hill, 1969.

Band, William A. *Creating Value for Customers: Designing and Implementing a Total Corporate Strategy*. New York: Wiley, 1991.

Barker, Joel A. *Discovering the Future: The Business of Paradigms*. 2d ed. Burnsville, Minn.: Infinity and Charthouse, 1989. Video.

———. *Paradigm Pioneers*. Discovering the Future Series. Burnsville, Minn.: Charthouse, 1993. Video.

Beacham, Walton, Richard T. Hise, and Hale N. Tongren. *Beacham's Marketing Reference*, vol. 2. Washington, D.C.: Research Publishing, 1986.

Beckhard, Richard. "The Healthy Organization: A Profile." In *The Organization of the Future*, edited by Frances Hesselbein, Marshall Goldsmith, and Richard Beckhard, 326–28. San Francisco: Jossey-Bass, 1997.

Block, Peter. *The Empowered Manager: Positive Political Skills at Work*. San Francisco: Jossey-Bass, 1989.

Childers, Thomas A., and Nancy A. Van House. *What's Good? Describing Your Public Library's Effectiveness*. Chicago: American Library Association, 1993.

Cornish, Edward, ed. *Exploring Your Future: Living, Learning, and Working in the Information Age.* Bethesda, Md.: World Future Society, 1996.

Covey, Stephen R., A. Roger Merrill, and Rebecca R. Merrill. *First Things First.* New York: Simon & Schuster, 1994.

Davis, Peter. "Libraries at the Turning Point: Issues in Proactive Planning." *Journal of Library Administration* 1, no. 2 (Summer 1980): 11–24.

Davis, Stann, and Christopher Meyer. *Blur: The Speed of Change in the Connected Economy.* Reading, Mass.: Addison-Wesley, 1998.

Dervin, Brenda. "Useful Theory for Librarianship: Communication, Not Information." *Drexel Library Quarterly* 13, no. 3 (July 1977): 24.

Despres, Ted, and Diane Driessen. *Writing Goals and Objectives, Long Range Planning for Public Libraries.* Occasional Paper Series 1, no. 5. Columbus, Ohio: State Library of Ohio, n.d.

Drucker, Peter F. *Management: Tasks, Responsibilities, Practices.* New York: Harper & Row, 1974.

The Futurist: A Magazine of Forecasts, Trends, and Ideas About the Future. Bethesda, Md.: The World Future Society, any issue.

Gray, Barbara. *Collaborating: Finding Common Ground for Multiparty Problems.* San Francisco: Jossey-Bass, 1989.

Hammer, Michael. "The Soul of the New Organization." In *The Organization of the Future,* edited by Frances Hesselbein, Marshall Goldsmith, and Richard Beckhard, 31. San Francisco: Jossey-Bass, 1997.

Hamon, Peter, Darlene E. Weingand, and Al Zimmerman. *Budgeting and the Political Process in Libraries: Simulation Games.* Englewood, Colo.: Libraries Unlimited, 1992.

Hardy, James M. *Corporate Planning for Nonprofit Organizations.* New York: Association Press, 1972.

Hesselbein, Frances, and others. *The Organization of the Future.* San Francisco: Jossey-Bass, 1997.

Himmel, Ethel, and William James Wilson. *Planning for Results: A Public Library Transformation Process.* Chicago: American Library Association, 1998.

Houle, Cyril O. *The Design of Education.* San Francisco: Jossey-Bass, 1976.

———. "Evidence for the Effectiveness of Continuing Professional Education and the Impact of Mandatory Continuing Education." In *Proceedings: Mandatory Continuing Education: Prospects and Dilemmas for Professionals,* edited by Donald E. Moore, Jr., 124. Urbana, Ill.: University of Illinois Press, 1976.

Hussey, David E. *Introducing Corporate Planning.* 2d ed. New York: Pergamon Press, 1979.

Hutchinson, John G. *Management Strategy and Tactics.* New York: Holt, Rinehart & Winston, 1971.

Jaugstetter, Mike, and Janice Williams. *Strategy Development and Evaluation, Long Range Planning for Public Libraries.* Occasional Paper Series 1, no. 6. Columbus, Ohio: State Library of Ohio, n.d.

Johnson Wilcox, Debra. "Training Outlines and Guidelines." In Douglas Zweizig and others, *The TELL IT! Manual: The Complete Program for Evaluating Library Performance,* 70. Chicago: American Library Association, 1996.

Kaplan, Robert E. *Beyond Ambition: How Driven Managers Can Lead Better and Live Better.* San Francisco: Jossey-Bass, 1991.

Kotler, Philip. *Marketing for Nonprofit Organizations.* Englewood Cliffs, N.J.: Prentice-Hall, 1975.

———. *Marketing for Nonprofit Organizations.* 2d ed. Englewood Cliffs, N.J.: Prentice-Hall, 1982.

Kotler, Philip, and Alan R. Andreasen. *Strategic Marketing for Nonprofit Organizations.* 3d ed. Englewood Cliffs, N.J.: Prentice-Hall, 1987.

Kubik, George. "Future Views: External Environmental Scanning." *Future Trends* 28:2 (March/April 1997): 1.

Lipman-Blumen, Jean. *The Connective Edge: Leading in an Interdependent World.* San Francisco: Jossey-Bass, 1996.

Mathews, Anne J. "The Use of Marketing Principles in Library Planning." In *Marketing for Libraries and Information Agencies,* edited by Darlene E. Weingand, 12. Norwood, N.J.: Ablex, 1984.

McClure, Charles R., and others. *Planning and Role Setting for Public Libraries: A Manual of Options and Procedures.* Chicago: American Library Association, 1987.

Nadler, David A., and others. *Discontinuous Change: Leading Organizational Transformation.* San Francisco: Jossey-Bass, 1995.

Newcomb, J. "Electronic Information Distribution." *Special Libraries* 74, no. 2 (April 1983): 155.

Palmour, Vernon E., Marcia C. Bellassai, and Nancy V. DeWath. *A Planning Process for Public Libraries.* Chicago: American Library Association, 1980.

Riggs, Donald E. *Strategic Planning for Library Managers.* Phoenix, Ariz.: Oryx Press, 1984.

Robbins-Carter, Jane, and Douglas L. Zweizig. "Are We There Yet?" *American Libraries* 16, no. 9 (October 1985): 624.

Rogers, Everett M., and F. Floyd Shoemaker. *Communication of Innovations, A Cross Cultural Approach.* 2d ed. New York: Free Press, 1971.

Rosenberg, Philip. *Cost Finding for Public Libraries: A Manager's Handbook.* Chicago: American Library Association, 1985.

Ross, Judith B. "New Strategies: Price and the Behavioral Learning Model." In *Marketing Public Library Services: New Strategies,* compiled by Darlene E. Weingand, 59. Chicago: American Library Association, 1985.

Salzman, Marian, and Ira Matathia. "Lifestyles of the Next Millennium: 65 Forecasts." *The Futurist* 32, no. 5 (June/July 1998), special insert.

Schmidt, Warren H., and Jerome P. Finnigan. *The Race Without a Finish Line: America's Quest for Total Quality.* San Francisco: Jossey-Bass, 1992.

Schwartz, Peter. *The Art of the Long View: Planning for the Future in an Uncertain World.* New York: Currency Doubleday, 1996.

Slaughter, Richard A. *Futures: Tools & Techniques.* Melbourne, Australia: Futures Study Centre and DDM Media Group, 1995.

Snyder, Herbert. "Allocating Costs: Is It a Program Worth Keeping?" *Library Administration & Management* 12, no. 3 (Summer 1998): 167.

Steiner, George A. *The "How" of Strategic Planning*. New York: AMACOM, 1978.

Sterngold, Arthur. "Marketing for Special Libraries and Information Centers: The Positioning Process." *Special Libraries* 73, no. 4 (October 1982): 254–59.

Tjosvold, Dean. *Teamwork for Customers: Building Organizations That Take Pride in Serving*. San Francisco: Jossey-Bass, 1993.

Vaill, Peter B. *Managing As a Performing Art: New Ideas for a World of Change*. San Francisco: Jossey-Bass, 1991.

Weingand, Darlene E. *Customer Service Excellence: A Concise Guide for Librarians*. Chicago: American Library Association, 1997.

———. "Distribution of the Library's Product: The Need for Innovation." *Journal of Library Administration* 4, no. 4 (Winter 1984): 49–57.

———. *Future-Driven Library Marketing*. Chicago: American Library Association, 1998.

———. *Managing Today's Public Library: Blueprint for Change*. Englewood, Colo.: Libraries Unlimited, 1994.

———. *The Organic Public Library*. Littleton, Colo.: Libraries Unlimited, 1984.

Weingand, Darlene E., ed. *Library Trends: Marketing of Library and Information Services* 43, no. 3 (Winter 1995).

Wilkins, Wallace. "Overcoming Fear of the Unknown." *The Futurist* 32:7 (October 1998): 60.

Zachert, M. J. K. "The Design of Special Library Teaching Tools." *Special Libraries* 64, no. 9 (September 1973): 362.

Zweizig, Douglas, and others. *The TELL IT! Manual: The Complete Program for Evaluating Library Performance*. Chicago: American Library Association, 1996.

INDEX

182 Ꮖ Index

Opportunities, marketing audit, 43
Organization
  activity analysis, marketing
      audit, 52–53
  assets of, marketing audit, 50
  "healthy," 166–68
  internal environment of, 5, 14,
      15, 15fig, 17fig, 48–50
  liabilities of, marketing audit, 50
  marketing activity in, 5, 50–52
  objectives, 4
  resources expended, 63
  structure of, 49
Outlets for place, 125–26
Outsourcing, 124–25
Ownership
  of goals, 62
  of team's process, 22–23

Palmour, Vernon, 12
Participative versus autocratic
    team structure, 22
Patrons versus customers, xii, xiv,
    82
Perception of benefit as motivator
    for planning, 11
Periodic marketing audit, 42
Personal contact, promotion by, 137
Personalizing the service, promo-
    tion by, 138–39
Personnel
  costs, 107, 109
  management goals, 60
  place, factor of, 124–25
  time and planning, 11
Pilot approach for action strategies,
    76
PIP (public information plan), 140–42
PLA (Public Library Association),
    32, 33fig, 34fig
Place (distribution), 115–32
  access, affected by, 119
  atmospherics for outlets, 125, 138
  change factor, 128–29
  channels of distribution, 115–19,
      117fig
  convenience factor, 119, 121–23,
      125–26

decision factors, 119–30, 120fig
delivery factor, 126–28
direct costs, 106, 106fig
distribution, placing the product,
    130–31
format factor, 126–27
and 4 Ps relationship, 117–19
and goals relationship, 118
human resource intermediaries
    factor, 124–25
innovation factor, 128–29
jobbers, 124–25
life cycle factor, 129
marketing audit for, 53, 116,
    117fig, 125, 130
in marketing/planning process,
    7, 16, 17fig
and mission statement relation-
    ship, 118
and objectives relationship, 118
operations-based quality, 121
outlets, number and location,
    factor, 125–26
outsourcing, 124–25
and planning relationship, 117–19
positioning factor, 130
and price (cost) relationship, 118
priorities factor, 123
and product relationship, 117–18
product transmittal outlets, 125
product-based quality, 121
and promotion relationship, 118
quality of service factor, 120–21
resource allocation factor, 121–23
scenario for, 131
stakeholder management, 123–24
technology delivery factor, 126–28
time factor, 121–23
transcendent quality, 121
tree concept of, 116, 117fig
user-based quality, 121
value-based quality, 121
vendors, 124–25
Planning philosophy, 9–13. See
    also Marketing and infor-
    mation management;
    Marketing/planning merger
  actions for, 10
  as an exchange relationship, 11